SIR FRANCIS BACON'S
OWN STORY

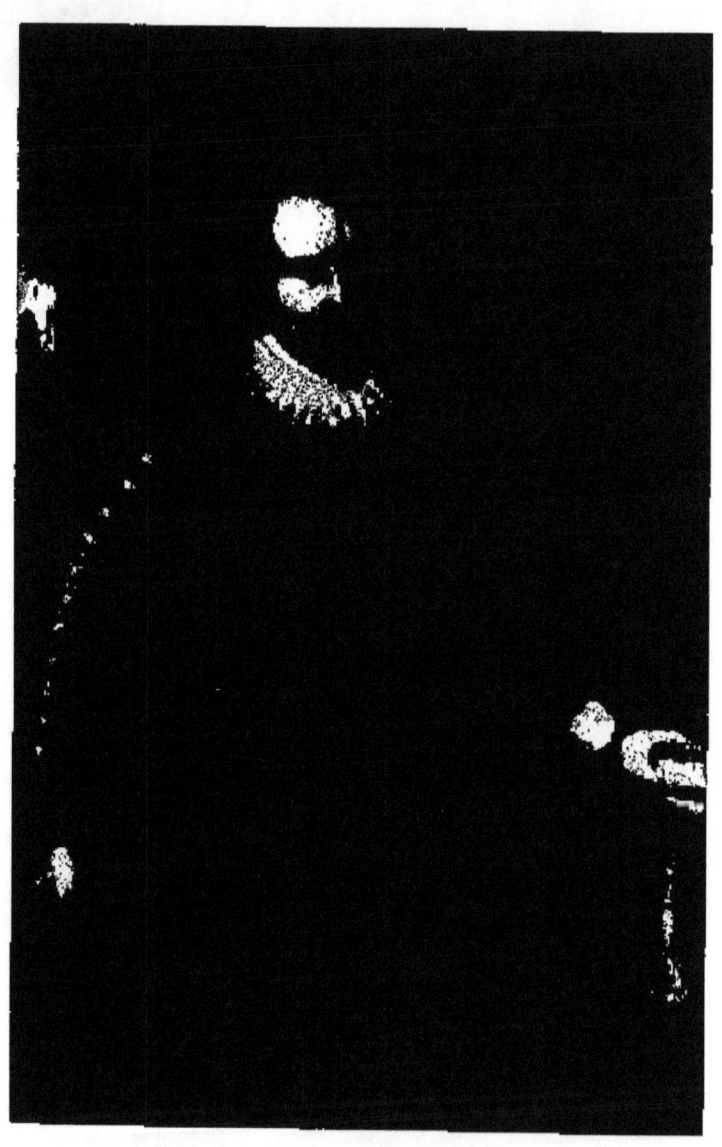

SIR FRANCIS BACON'S OWN STORY

BY

J. E. ROE

AUTHOR OF
"BACON AND HIS MASKS
THE DEFOE PERIOD UNMASKED"

"I have (though in a despised weed) procured the good of all men"—*Francis St. Alban*

BY THE AUTHOR
The DuBois Press
Rochester, N. Y.

Copyright 1918
BY
J. E. ROE

FEB 20 1918

CONTENTS

                                                                                 PAGE

SIR FRANCIS BACON'S OWN STORY COMPLETE IN FIVE CHAPTERS . . . .

A FOREWORD, OR RELATIONAL FACTS—*The Mission* 3

INTRODUCTION 6

DOOR OF ENTRANCE 12

CHAPTER I. Was Francis Bacon a concealed poet? Did he write Sonnets concerning Queen Elizabeth? His covert Shakespeare Sonnets touching her successor. Had he personal interest in this succession? His struggle with the royal "Will," the will of Elizabeth while seeking official position. Coke his great rival placed in his stead. . . . 17

CHAPTER II. Francis Bacon's Overthrow, his impeachment and fall, and his dealings with his sovereign or King, James 1st, during and following that event, as set forth in his Shakespeare Sonnets. 26

CHAPTER III. Francis Bacon's wonder. His new inductive or tabular system of philosophy. That something absolutely new of the Shakespeare Sonnet 59, and its eternized "tables" of Sonnet 122, and its "great bases for eternity" of Sonnets 124 and 125; in other words his "new born child;" his "Noblest Birth of Time." These "tables" were to bear his name to future ages, and make him long outlive "that idle rank" which downed him. 48

CHAPTER IV. Shake-speare, Bacon's cover; his "noted weed" of Sonnet 76. His two Sonnet Sentinels—the T. T. Enigma and the 1609 Ante-date. The true causes involved in his overthrow. His "second life on second head" of Sonnet 68. His Posthumous Pocket labors. The Carlyle waifs from the Bacon budget. He remained long, long at labor. Was in concealment from and after 1626. As covert secretary and mouth-piece to Cromwell and the Independents, he was behind the great struggle that put Charles 1st from the English throne. If Elizabeth's rightful successor, was he not England's lawful King? His "Holy War," his "Pilgrim's Progress," his "Milton." . 80

CHAPTER V. The field of Invention. Relation of the sciences to Poetry. Cyphers of both literary periods. The undisclosed Overall cypher of the second. This the true Key. The "Sartor Resartus," Bacon's work of durance. Contains it the "Alphabet?" 190

RELATIONAL FACTS

Touching his greatest discovery, his "Alphabet of Nature," or the discovery of forms, Bacon says: "He is an ill discoverer who thinks there is no land when he can see nothing but sea."

The value he, himself, set upon this "Alphabet" of forms—laws of "the simple natures"—he states thus: "Such then is the rule and plan of the alphabet. May God the Maker, the Preserver, the Renewer of the universe, of his love and compassion to man protect and guide this work, both in its ascent to His glory, and in its descent to the good of man, through His only Son, God with us."

This "Alphabet," his "Noblest Birth of Time," was to be revealed only through or by means of his "Formula of Interpretation," be it remembered; for intended concealment, as well as confusion, has long lurked here, baffling all of his critics. This "Formula" this key, Reader, was to be his only heir.

Speaking of his great felt mission, Francis Bacon, himself, says: "I have taken all knowledge to be my providence."

He undertook to exercise a "providence"—note the word—over all human learning. See this scope portrayed in his "New Atlantis" with its twelve heads, and one concealed. In its closing paragraph we have: "I give thee leave to publish it for the good of other nations, for we are here in God's bosom a land unknown." He believed the human body to be nature's apex, and nature to be God's art, and the human mind, to be the seat of providence.

In his Shakespeare Plays, he was at labor in the wilderness. And in Hamlet, of his great mission, says: "The time is out of joint, O, cursed spite that ever I was born to set it right."

In his "Novum Organum"—New Organ—he was at labor upon that something absolutely new, his tabular system of philosophy, and of it, says: "Nay, it is a point fit and necessary in the front and beginning of this work, without hesitation or reservation to be professed, that it is not less true in this human kingdom of knowledge than in God's kingdom of Heaven, that no man shall enter into it except he become first as a little child." At its completion and publication he called it, "my new born child," as we shall see. While yet in its swaddlings, before publication, he in Hamlet refers to it as: "That great baby you see there is not yet out of his swaddling-clouts."

In his labors on theology, he, in the introductory pages to his "New Organ," says: "Having completed by a rigorous levy a complete host of divine works, nothing remains to be done but to attack philosophy itself." We echo and re-echo to you, Reader, the question: What became of these divine works?

As to labors touching government, he in 1623 says: "If I should hereafter have leisure to write upon government, the work will probably be either posthumous or abortive." Concerning concealment of method, he says: "The glory of God is to conceal a thing, but the glory of the king is to find it out; as if, according to the innocent play of children, the Divine Majesty took delight to hide his works to the end to have them found out; and as if Kings could not obtain greater honor than to be God's play-fellows in that game."

Bacon's brooding note rests here. He imitated the divine plan throughout his works. His "New Organ" was but the tabernacle in which his key, his "Formula of Interpretation," was to be the Ark. This key, this "Formula" was by design never placed. It was reserved to a private succession as will hereafter appear from his own words. We are now and here in search of it, Reader. By the foregoing we would assist the reader's apprehension in grasping, at the outset, the covert nature of the Baconian mission.

INTRODUCTION

IN a literary sense, whoever follows Francis Bacon feeds at the highest line of the world's literature. This is as true to-day, as it was two centuries ago. His matchless ideation and cogency of reason, were never equalled. These proclaim him the world's literary master, and in a sense not yet made manifest, as we shall see. We agree with Macaulay that the amplitude of his comprehension was never yet vouchsafed to any other human being. This it was that gave character to his vast reform, its subtlety of execution, and its never before attempted method of introduction. Its key-note, using his own words, was: "Without the help of the knowledge of evil, virtue remains open and unfenced."

With his views the deeps of Satan should be all known to him who would be the true instructor, as we shall see later from his own words. We shall also see, that he undertook to exercise a providence over all human learning, and in this, among other things, reports a history of literature wanting.

We here set you up a point, Reader. Let it be retained, please, throughout the reading of this work, to wit, "a history of literature is wanting." To supply this was but part of his great Posthumous Pocket labors.

While throughout, as in his Plays, entertainment of the mind was to be the lever, the help of the knowledge of evil was to be the fulcrum, to lift the age to a higher level.

We shall here invite the attention of the student of English literature to something new; and which will render it more easy, both of apprehension and retention.

But whatever we may do in this work, we desire above all else to make it clear, that Francis Bacon's key, his "Formula of Interpretation," this new light, was never revealed by him while living, but was reserved to a private succession, as we shall see.

Following his fall, he says: "I shall devote myself to letters, instruct the actors and serve posterity. In such a course, I shall perhaps find honor and I shall pass my life as within the verge of a better." These actors were factors of his pen. They were his facets of light. They were his "hands of my hands." Their doings, Reader, were to come out from the "cabinets, boxes and presses" named in his last will.

When his story, the covert story of Elizabeth's successor has been rightly told; it will not appear as strangely as now, that he ended not his earthly career by death at the Earl of Arundel's house, as now generally supposed; but was covertly behind that great struggle which put Charles 1st from the English throne. We come to you in this work, Reader, with a new message. We shall endeavor, in the main, to give Bacon's words throughout leaving the reader to his own conclusions. Upon the thread of his life we shall find, among others, his Shakespeare Sonnets, his Plays, his dream drama,—"The Pilgrim's Progress,"—his "Holy War," his "History of the Devil," his "Milton," his "Tale of a Tub," addressed to posterity, and that work of durance his "Sartor Resartus." And "the river of his history" will long bear them up.

Into this literary carcass, we shall now make entrance through those adroitly prepared tell-tales, known as the Shakespeare Sonnets. Having shown in the work itself, that "that eternity promised" by Francis Bacon to his "noted weed,"—his Shakespeare,—in the Enigma found upon their title page, subscribed T. T.; was fulfilled to the letter in Sonnet 81; and that he made both Shakespeare's epitaph and monument; we here and now permit him in his own chosen words in Sonnets 88, 89 and 90, to tell the reader the circumstances connected with that strange and most striking feature of his career, his own personal overthrow. And so to King James in Sonnet 88 Bacon says:

> WHEN thou shalt be disposed to set me light
> And place my merit in the eye of scorn,
> Upon thy side against myself I'll fight
> And prove thee virtuous, though thou art forsworn.
> With mine own weakness being best acquainted,
> Upon thy part I can set down a story
> Of faults conceal'd, wherein I am attainted,
> That thou in losing me shalt win much glory:
> And I by this will be a gainer too;
> For bending all my loving thoughts on thee,
> The injuries that to myself I do,
> Doing thee vantage, double-vantage me.
>   Such is my love, to thee I so belong,
>   That for thy right myself will bear all wrong."

The writer of this Sonnet has, in the Sonnets, so clearly particularized the points involved in his own personal overthrow as to need little comment to those familiar with that event. See Sonnets 89 and 90. Note "purposed overthrow" in Sonnet 90.

But were these three Sonnets addressed to a king? If doubted, see please Sonnets 57 and 58. In Sonnet 57 we have, "Whilst I, my sovereign, watch the clock for you." That the overthrow was acquiesced in, to shield the King, see Sonnet 125. That the submission was upon the King's urgent advice, see Sonnet 49. That there was an interview with the King for the purpose, see please Sonnet 113. As to the King's pretended sorrow, sympathy, and tears, see Sonnets 34 and 35. That they were "Siren tears" see later Sonnet 119. That the author was made "tongue-tied" before his shearers, see Sonnets 66 and 140. That "needy nothing trimm'd in jollity" of Sonnet 66 was, we say Buckingham, the then King's favorite. Shaksper? Ha!

Reader, has not ignorance long enough been made to o'er-crow, and crown the brow, of the best literature of modern times? If not, then let our wise lauder, not of culture, but the crow, still make manifest to the literary world, if he can, Shaksper's authorship of the foregoing Sonnet, yea Sonnets.

We stay for his performance. We challenge it. He shall not longer escape by jumps. While waiting, we would suggest to the reader something new, yes New! concerning the envy and overthrow of this great genius; of whom Macaulay says: "With great minuteness of observation, he had an amplitude of comprehension that was never yet vouchsafed to any other human being."

Among private notes, in Greek, made subsequent to his fall, Bacon says: "My story is proud."

Though nearly three centuries have passed, that story, the true story, of Francis Bacon's overthrow, has not been told, Reader. We say it has not! We will yet tell it, first in the Sonnets, then in the facts of his history in Chapter 4, space forbids it here. Bacon himself alludes to it, cautiously, in the "several plot" of that subtle Sonnet 137. The King's hypnotism over him had ceased, at the writing of Sonnets 118, 140 and 147, let it be remembered. Make now these four Sonnets into Shaksper pabulum, you who can. Shaksper was the player, Shakespeare the nom de plume. The numbering of the Sonnets was but part of their method of concealment, as was their Enigma, their ante-date and their pronoun cover words.

Come ye men of culture, having received the dope of literary domination, and snored for nearly three centuries, may not the new literary seed bed of Francis St. Alban now take air? If not, sleep on; the time will come when this restorer of ancient learning will have his due. He himself says: "So I seem to have my conversation among the ancients, more than among these with whom I live." Let this thought as to the ancients be retained by the reader through every stage of this work until we reach his "Classic Authors in Wood." "Men are made of wood," says Bacon. The Plays are his wood-notes of their doings. They represent the wilderness, the old witch; the world; and they were warbled wild, to be elsewhere expanded. Of that expansion we will tell you later, in connection with Francis Bacon's "second life on second head" of Sonnet 68 where the good days of Queen Elizabeth are contrasted with the "bastard signs of fair" of those of James the 1st.

The foregoing Sonnets now placed, as well as others, see Sonnet 121, will hereafter remain an enduring revelation upon this question of authorship. And we here throw wide the door.

Bacon's own dummy may now yield him place as the real author. It is for the welfare of literature that this be now done; for a new literary age will yet arise out of that "unseen sowing," that "second life on second head," be it remembered. We will endeavor later in the work itself to make clear the points here touched to relation, and especially concerning the overthrow. In the interest of justice, as well as of literature, this should now be done.

And we will perform it, we trust, to the satisfaction of careful thought. This, though brief, is our carefully prepared speech to posterity, concerning important historic events, that, to this hour, remain a cloud upon literature.

In this work our "Defoe Period Unmasked" will be made use of, as a work of reference, for the benefit of any who may desire a more extended information upon the facts that may be here given. It has not till now, save a few copies, been given to the public.

OUR DOOR OF ENTRANCE

We here call to relation and division the never before interpreted Shakespeare Sonnets, reserving Bacon's Posthumous Pocket labors for the later portion of the work.

The 154 scholastic compendiums of Francis Bacon, known as the Shakespeare Sonnets, having remained the world's literary puzzle for nearly three centuries, we thought it commendable to make further trial of their opening. After much careful research we found them to be covert tell-tales, not of the player Shaksper, but of Francis Bacon, their real author; and have called them into the divisions following.

I. All of the Shakespeare Sonnets from 1 to 19 have a covert reference to succession. See Sonnets 2, 3 and 4. That they concern a Prince, and do not concern a private person, see, please, Sonnet 14, then 7 and 9. They were designed to suggest to Queen Elizabeth the importance to truth, of a Protestant heir, by her, to the English throne. See in this, please, the prognostication of Sonnet 14. The Catholic Mary Queen of Scots was, at the time, her successor. Elizabeth was the last of the House of Tudor. She had formed a fixed determination against marriage as is well known. This then was to leave vacant the English throne of Protestant heirs. This determination against marriage appears in several of these Sonnets; and in Sonnet 13 she is asked not to let "so fair a house fall to decay" and alluding to her father Henry 8th, the author says to her, "you had a father, let your son say so." Had Francis Bacon any interest in this succession, Reader? Was he a concealed poet? Did he himself write Sonnets concerning the Queen? We shall see.

II. A portion concerns their author's struggle with the royal "Will;" the will of Queen Elizabeth while seeking official position, his great rival being placed in his stead. See Sonnets 133 to 137 also 143 and 145.

Let the capitalized "Will" in Sonnets 135, 136 and 143 be carefully noted, as it is claimed to allude to the player's name Will. Will Shaksper. We submit that careful thought can never apply this word "Will," as here used, to the name of any individual. In Sonnet 143 the author alludes to the Queen as his mother, and to himself as her babe chasing her far behind, seeking his will through hers, and in Sonnet 135 asks her, for once, at least, to hide his will in hers. See in this, please, "Bacon's Letters" Vol. 1, page 359; then see page 347 and 348. That the Queen really was his mother; see the subtlety of Sonnet 22. When he said to her in Sonnet 20 "And by addition me of thee defeated" referred he to Essex? See "Essex" in Bacon's cypher story. As this subject concerns the Queen, so we consider it with division 1 in our First Chapter.

III. A portion of them concerns their author's own individual troubles, his impeachment and fall; and his dealings with his sovereign, or King, James 1st, during and following that event.

IV. A portion concerns that wonder, their author's tabular system of philosophy, that something absolutely new of Sonnet 59, and its "tables" of Sonnet 122 and its blessed key of Sonnet 52, and its "great bases for eternity" of Sonnets 124 and 125. These "tables" were to bear the author's name to future ages, and make him long outlive "that idle rank" that downed him.

V. A portion of them concerns their author's "noted weed" of Sonnet 76; his nom de plume; in other words, his hyphened name Shake-speare. Most of the quartos have a hyphen between the words Shake and speare. The player's name was Shaksper. Following his fall, in a carefully written prayer, Bacon says: "I have (though in a despised weed) procured the good of all men." We understand him here to allude to those thought patterns his Shakespeare plays.

VI. A portion of them concerns a new life by their author upon a new or "second head," as stated in Sonnet 68, where the good days of Queen Elizabeth are contrasted with the "bastard signs of fair" of those of James 1st under whom he met his overthrow. This Sonnet must ever form the line of demarkation between Francis Bacon's first and second literary periods. This division will be considered in connection with division 5, in our 4th chapter.

VII. A portion of them concerns praise of their author's own mental gifts as notably in Sonnets 53 and 122 and of his philosophy or greatly felt mission; as in Sonnet 59 but which praise, or "self-love," he later much condemns in himself in Sonnet 62 which ends thus:

"'Tis thee, myself, that for myself I praise
Pointing my age with beauty of thy days."

Note here the words "thee," "myself." This is the first and only Sonnet that gives the key to their author's method of cover words used in them. This should be studied with some care as it is used in other portions of Bacon's non-attributed work. He here shows that the pronoun "thee" refers to himself, and is in this a disclosed cover word. The author preserved his manners in not openly praising himself, by use of these pronoun cover words here considered. He describes his method in the

THE NEW AGE

above quotation in the words, "'Tis thee, myself, that for myself I praise."

Under this division of the Sonnets the pronouns, "thee," "thy," "thou," "you," "he," "his," "him" and "himself" and others are used as cover words wherein the author alludes to himself, or to his own intelligence. To instance, in the words, "you" and "your," in Sonnet 53, the author lauds his own mental gifts. In the same words, "you" and "your," he alludes to himself in Sonnet 55. He does this in Sonnets 67 and 68 in the words, "he," "his" and "him." By "him" in Sonnet 19 the author breathes the wish that he might be "beauty's pattern to succeeding men," but would be so, note the word, "untainted."

This use of pronouns in the second and third person instead of the first, as a cover to conceal the author's identity, was made use of by Dante, Homer, and Horace. Dante in excusing himself for it says: "In Horace, man is made to speak to his own intelligence as unto another person; and not only hath Horace done this, but herein he followeth the excellent Homer." This must ever be the first postulate in a correct interpretation of the Sonnets which fall under this division. Careful study of their context will show whether the author alludes to philosophy as in Sonnet 29 and 37 or to king, queen or himself.

In scope, all of the Sonnets may properly be herded under one or the other of the foregoing divisions.

FRANCIS BACON'S OWN STORY

CHAPTER I

WAS FRANCIS BACON A CONCEALED POET? WROTE HE SONNETS CONCERNING QUEEN ELIZABETH? HIS COVERT SHAKESPEARE SONNETS TOUCHING HER SUCCESSOR. HAD HE PERSONAL INTEREST IN THIS SUCCESSION? HIS STRUGGLE WITH HER ROYAL "WILL" FOR OFFICIAL POSITION.

THAT Francis Bacon was a concealed poet, he, himself shall tell you, reader. He says: "All history, excellent King, treads the earth performing the duty of a guide, rather than a light, and poetry is, as it were, the stream of knowledge." See Invention and the relation of poetry to the sciences at the opening of Chapter 5.

It will be said this but shows the value Bacon set upon the "stream"—the ancient poets—for light, for information; and in no way shows him to have been a performer in, or writer of, poetry. True; yet this is a legitimate step, we think, to the platform intended, which says, Sir Francis Bacon was a "dark author;" a concealed poet, the scope and subtlety of whose gifts have never been surpassed.

At the accession of the Scotch King, James, to the English throne, at the death of Elizabeth in 1603, Bacon addressed a careful letter to his literary friend, Sir John Davis, desiring him to interest himself in his, Bacon's behalf, with the incoming King, and he closes the letter thus: "So desiring you to be good to concealed poets, I continue your very assured. Fr. Bacon."

Comes he not here upon our platform, reader? If, then, Francis Bacon was a concealed poet, by his own showing, ought we to expect him to put this in flourish, upon pages of his attributed writings? Or in any place? Surely not.

Mr. Spedding, in a foot-note to the letter, says: "The allusion to concealed poets I cannot explain." That the letter forbids any other interpretation, than the one given, see "Bacon's Letters" by Spedding (Vol. 3, p. 65).

But again, did Francis Bacon employ his pen, as a poet, in Sonnet writing; and particularly in Sonnets concerning the Queen? He shall tell. He says: "A little before that time, being about the middle of Michaelmas term, her Majesty had a purpose to dine at my lodge at Twicknam Park, at which time I had (though I profess not to be a poet) prepared a Sonnet directly tending and alluding to draw on her Majesty's reconcilement to my Lord." "Bacon's Letters," Vol. 3, p. 149. Of the Queen he says: "She suffered herself, and was very willing to be courted, wooed, and to have sonnets made in her commendation; and she continued this longer than was decent for her years."

We now present the reader an example of Francis Bacon's poetic skill, in a Sonnet concededly written by him, touching Queen Elizabeth, and quote from "Bacon's Letters" by Spedding, Vol. 1, p. 388, thus:

"Seated between the Old World and the New,
 A land there is no other land may touch,
 Where reigns a Queen in peace and honor true;
 Stories or fables do describe no such.
 Never did Atlas such a burden bear,
 As she, in holding up the world opprest;
 Supplying with her virtue everywhere
 Weakness of friends, errors of servants best.

No nation breeds a warmer blood for war,
And yet she calms them by her majesty;
No age hath ever wits refined so far,
And yet she calms them by her policy;
To her, thy son must make his sacrifice
If he will have the morning of his eyes."

Few, we think, are aware of the existence of this Sonnet, or of the occasion which called it forth. We would place it. Let the style, structure and literary merit of this Sonnet, this talker in verse, be drawn into direct relation and studious comparison with every, and each, of the Shakespeare Sonnets, so called, beginning with the laudation of the Queen in Sonnet 106, where we have:

WHEN in the chronicle of wasted time
I see descriptions of the fairest wights,
And beauty making beautiful old rhyme
In praise of ladies dead and lovely knights,
Then, in the blazon of sweet beauty's best,
Of hand, of foot, of lip, of eye, of brow,
I see their antique pen would have express'd
Even such a beauty as you master now.
So all their praises are but prophecies
Of this our time, all you prefiguring;
And, for they look'd but with divining eyes,
They had not skill enough your worth to sing:
 For we, which now behold these present days,
 Have eyes to wonder, but lack tongues to praise."

Here is your opportunity, reader, your tentative Example. You may here contrast the obverse and reverse, or the light and dark side of this great genius, this interpreter of the ancients, this literary mint. Shaksper? Ha!

Already the cover—the nom de plume—has served its purpose. The unmasking comes more easily in the Sonnets, than in the Plays.

Bacon's special praise of the Queen will be found not merely in the mentioned Shakespeare Sonnet 106, but most notably in Act V., Scene IV, of his play of "Henry the Eighth." Fail not reader to see there, please, what he says concerning her successor. The writer of the plays a Catholic? This particularized prophesy and noble laudation as to the infant Elizabeth in Henry the 8th make it certain that he was not. Though the last of the House of Tudor, she had formed a fixed determination against marriage. All of the Shakespeare Sonnets, from 1 to 19, concern Elizabeth and succession. They are designed to suggest to her the importance to truth of an heir to the English throne, through her. That the mentioned eighteen Sonnets concern a Prince, and do not concern a private person, see Sonnets 7 and 9, and particularly Sonnet 14, which prognosticates danger to truth, and extinction of the Queen's beauty, if she fails of issue; that is, to "convert" herself "to store." See the Sonnet. The author in Sonnet 13, clearly alludes to the House of Tudor, and urges upon the Queen not to let "so fair a house fall to decay." He there likewise alludes to her father, Henry the Eighth, and says to her: "You had a father; let your son say so."

It is for the thinker we design this work, and he will find himself rewarded by careful examination of the references given.

If now Bacon was really the son of Leicester and the Queen, by a valid, secret marriage, as claimed in his own Bi-literal Cypher Story, presented in Mrs. Gallup's wonderful book; then may these purposeful eighteen Sonnets be justly regarded as an adroit urging upon the Queen to declare or proclaim his own lawful right to the throne, as her successor; well knowing at the time her years forbid issue, and that she could not, or would not, wed. As she could not be induced to do this, so in Sonnet 68 "the right of sepulchres were shorn away." Do Sonnets 22 and 143 concern mother and son? Let it now be observed that our first quoted Sonnet ends in significant words. The word, in parentheses touching the father, Leicester, is ours.

"To her, thy son (Leicester), must make his sacrifice,
If he will have the morning of his eyes."

Bacon, to Elizabeth, did make the sacrifice, as we shall see; and he did thereby, for a time, get "the morning of his eyes." This Sonnet, let it be noted, was written by Francis Bacon, as part of a mask, to be played before the Queen, following his long tentative struggle with her, for the office, first, of attorney-general, and then of solicitor; and, of her final rejection of him in both instances, after a dalliance of upwards of two years. (Bacon's Letters, Vol. 1, p. 369 and 370).

The history of the event will show that she had induced him to believe that he was to receive the appointment. (Bacon's Letters, Vol. 1, p. 359. See on p. 348, what he says of the Queen's willfulness in the matter). Earlier, by a speech in Parliament, he had offended her; and would not, or at least had not, retracted or apologized. We here claim to the reader that during this, Bacon's greatest, yea, his only struggle with the Queen, the notable Shakespeare Sonnets 135, 136 and 143 were written. They belong with our 2nd Division of the Sonnets.

As the word "Will," in the three Sonnets, begins with a capital, it is said to stand for Will Shaksper. Here rests the most conspicuous argument for his authorship. We say that by no just theory of interpretation can the word be tortured to stand for the name of any individual. In each instance the word refers to the human will, and here stands for the royal Will, the will of Queen Elizabeth, and hence capitalized. "Best we lay a straw here," says Bacon in his Promus Note 108.

The Queen is represented in Sonnet 136 to be so willful that her love, her very being, centers in, and stands for, "Will." So the author says, if she will make his name to stand for her love, it will then be Will. That this interpretation cannot be justly questioned, see Sonnet 135. In Sonnets 133 and 134, he is said, through his friend, to be mortgaged to her will. The history of the event shows that the Queen forbade Bacon to come into her presence, and Sonnet 136 opens thus:

"If thy soul check thee that I come so near,
 Swear to thy blind soul that I was thy Will,
 And will, thy soul knows, is admitted there."

All of the Shakespeare Sonnets are concise talkers, talkers in verse, let it be remembered. Though subtle, when the event to which they belong is found, they are in full accord. Everywhere in them we have Bacon's vocabulary. The struggle with the Queen having ended, she, through Essex, made good his losses. Thus he found "the morning of his eyes." Then came Sonnet 145, and the dutiful submission elegantly portrayed to her, in the subtle mask wherein our quoted Sonnet forms but a part. In it will be found a touch of Bacon's secret mission against Spain or the Castilians.

Returning now to the use of the words, "Of hand, of foot, of lip, of eye, of brow," in Sonnet 106, and to the probabilities that it concerns the Queen and Bacon's authorship, we, from "Bacon's Letters" by Spedding, Vol. 1, page 138 quote him thus: "For the beauty and many graces of her presence, what colours are fine enough for such a portraiture? Let no light poet be used for such a description but the chastest and royalest. Of her gait, of her voice, of her eye, of her colour, of her neck, of her breast, of her hair. If this be presumption, let him bear the blame that oweth the verses." Stay, here please reader, a moment for reflection. That Bacon wrote Sonnets concerning the Queen clearly appears from his own words.

In Sonnet 15 he tells her that by his pen, he engrafts her new as Time takes from her. But in Sonnet 16 he returns to the ruling idea involved in the first eighteen Sonnets, to wit, the covert subject of succession. The author in this Sonnet makes reference to his pen as "Time's pencil or my pupil pen." Was it Shaksper's pen, reader? It here seems proper to focalize attention upon Bacon's emphasis upon the subject of time and his distinctive use of the word as spread in the Sonnets, in the plays and throughout his writings. See, please, Sonnet 123. We find him using such expressions as, "The noblest birth of time," "The wrongs of time," "The injuries of time," "It drinketh too much time," "To entertain the time," "Time is as a river." But in this brief outlining we must not stay upon the language features. In this, see the footnotes to our "Defoe Period." Note our purpose in them at p. 30.

When, touching his believed-in mission Bacon said, "I have taken all knowledge to be my providence;" he of it also said; "This, whether it be curiosity, or vain glory, or nature, or (if one take it favorably) philanthropia, is so fixed in my mind as it cannot be removed." See, please, "Bacon's Letters" by Spedding, Vol. 1, pages 108 and 109; or our "Defoe Period" pages 24 to 27 and 21 to 24.

This undated letter to his kinsman Burghley, then High Treasurer of England, and drawn forth by his necessities at or near his mentioned struggle with the Queen, and, we think, immediately following that event, should be read in full, remembering that its word "province" is erroneously substituted for Bacon's word "providence" as elsewhere shown. See our "Defoe Period" p. 25, 27 and 76.

This letter we would place as a continuing Head-light to the great purposes which were in Bacon's mind at the age of thirty-one. In it he says to his kinsman: "I confess that I have as vast contemplative ends, as I have moderate civil ends, for I have taken all knowledge to be my providence." He also says if he will not assist him to some place in her Majesty's service, "I will sell the inheritance that I have, and purchase some lease of quick revenue, or some office of gain that shall be executed by deputy, and so give over all care of service, and become some sorry bookmaker or a true pioneer in that mine of truth which is said to lay so deep."

Let these thoughts, these fixed purposes be carefully remembered when we come later in Chapter 4 to his new seats of learning. He evidently believed that for England at least "Time's pencil" was in his hand. Let it likewise be remembered that whoever believes himself wiser than his neighbor has ever envy at the door. Prejudice? Where, reader, can be found a more hateful devil to human progress? How can there be a steady advancement of learning when the pseudo-literary domineer over and rule all. To break this domination and set free the intellect was the business of his new seats of learning, "his almost new features in the intellectual world," as we shall see later.

CHAPTER II

FRANCIS BACON'S OVERTHROW. HIS DEALINGS WITH HIS SOVEREIGN OR KING, JAMES 1ST, DURING AND FOLLOWING THAT EVENT, AS SET FORTH IN HIS SHAKESPEARE SONNETS.

AS Francis Bacon's overthrow was the strange and most striking feature of his career, so from this platform would we begin the work of shaking out the folds of his vast reform. After the lapse of nearly three hundred years, we permit Sir Francis Bacon to relate, in his own chosen words, the circumstances of his impeachment and fall. This we do in an examination of those of his Shakespeare Sonnets which concern the fall of their author; using but material sufficient to call them to relation with that strange event.

The Shakespeare Sonnets are guarded upon their title-page first by an ante-date 1609; and later by an Enigma subscribed T. T. These two Sentinels will be considered later in Chapter 4.

Suffice it here to say, that the Shakespeare Sonnets, as we now have them, were not in print prior to Bacon's fall in 1621. They have thus far been considered enigmatic as to any special design or purpose; and to be but poetic effusions, though great labor has been bestowed upon them. The noted Shakespearean, Grant White, says, "The mystery of the Shakespeare Sonnets will never be unfolded." Subtlety must therefore be looked for by the reader, who should assist in getting our points with the least number of words.

The difficulty has ever been in trying to place these garments where they can in no true sense be made to fit.

While drawing the Sonnets, as a whole, into several distinct heads, they having been written at different periods of their author's life, we purpose here to consider only those which concern his fall, and his dealings with his King—James I—during, and following that event. Its every detail, is, as we shall see, portrayed in them.

We trust, therefore, that the legal profession, which is our own, as well as the learned world generally, will be willing to be informed, even in verse, why the great St. Alban yielded to the King; and abandoned his defense.

This investigation will be found important in that, if right, it settles the whole question of authorship of plays, Sonnets, and other writings; and this without aid of key or cypher.

To make sure to the reader, at the outset, that the Sonnets to which we here refer, concern a King, or sovereign, we quote Sonnet 57 in full. Its author—was it Shaksper?—says to the King:

BEING your slave, what should I do but tend
Upon the hours and times of your desire?
I have no precious time at all to spend,
Nor services to do, till you require.
Nor dare I chide the world-without-end hour
Whilst I, my sovereign, watch the clock for you,
Nor think the bitterness of absence sour
When you have bid your servant once adieu;
Nor dare I question with my jealous thought
Where you may be, or your affairs suppose,
But, like a sad slave, stay and think of nought
Save, where you are how happy you make those.
  So true a fool is love that in your will,
  Though you do anything, he thinks no ill."

And what made the author of this Sonnet, whoever he was, the King's slave? It begins with "Being your slave" and Sonnet 58 opens with "What God forbid that made me first your slave." This we will tell the reader later in connection with Sonnet 120 in Chapter 4. We will there show when the King's secret hatred of Bacon became active. These Sonnets are in a sense, self reminders, soliloquies. Sonnets 57 and 58 were written while their author, Bacon, was waiting for, and expecting the King's promised pardon. The submissive attitude of a subject to his King, will appear in the words, "to thee I so belong," in Sonnet 88.

In Sonnets 58 and 87 the King's "charter" is directly alluded to. Bacon was his Chancellor at the time of his fall, and a "watchman ever for his sake," as stated in Sonnet 61. Note "image" as personating the King in this Sonnet. Bacon says: "I have borne your Majesty's image in metal, much more in heart." In Sonnet 48 note his good resolve taken when he was first made Chancellor. The "jewels" of this Sonnet concern the author's literary works as seen in Sonnets 52, 63, 64 and 65. In speaking of the structure of his great philosophic system, Bacon says, "I give thee the greatest jewel I have."

The history of Francis Bacon's impeachment and fall for bribery, while England's Chancellor, clearly shows that he was diligently preparing for his defense when he was sent for by the King; that an interview took place; that Bacon prepared minutes for it. "Bacon's Letters," vol. 7, page 235 where we have: "There be three degrees or cases of bribery charged or supposed in a judge:

1. The first, of bargain or contract for reward to pervert justice, pendente lite.

2. The second, where the Judge conceives the cause to be at an end by the information of the party, or otherwise, and useth not such diligence as he ought to inquire of it.

3. And the third when the cause is really ended, and it is sine fraude without relation to any precedent promise. Now if I might see the particulars of my charge, I should deal plainly with your Majesty, in whether of these degrees every particular case falls.

But for the first of them, I take myself to be as innocent as any born upon St. Innocent's day, in my heart.

For the second, I doubt in some particulars I may be faulty.

And for the last, I conceived it to be no fault, but therein I desire to be better informed, that I may be twice penitent, once for the fact, and again for the error. For I had rather be a briber, than a defender of bribes.

I must likewise confess to your Majesty that at new-years tides and likewise at my first coming in (which was as it were my wedding), I did not so precisely as perhaps I ought examine whether those that presented me had causes before me, yea or no."

He was Lord Keeper at the time he was made Chancellor. To this time it had been the custom, as Mr. Spedding informs us, of making gratuities or presents to the Chancellors. The charges against him were chiefly of that nature.

Earlier in a letter to the King, page 226, Bacon says, "I have been ever your man and counted myself but an usufructuary of myself, the property being yours; and now making myself an oblation to do with me as may best conduce to the honour of your justice, the honour of your mercy and the use of your service, resting as clay in your Majesty's gracious hands." In a later letter, page 241, he says, "This is the last suit I shall make to your Majesty in this business, prostrating myself at your mercy-seat, after fifteen year's service, wherein I have served your Majesty in my poor endeavors with an entire heart, and as I presumed to say unto your Majesty, am still a virgin for matters that concern your person or crown; and now only craving that after eight steps of honour I be not precipitated altogether."

That any attempted defense by Bacon at the time would have been folly, will be shown later in Chapter 4. For two years and more, pitfalls were being laid for him as we shall see.

Note in the foregoing his word "oblation" to the King. Note it then, to the King, in Sonnet 125. "Thou" in Sonnets 88, 89 and 90, alludes to him as we shall see. They ought all to be read studiously in relation with Bacon's words given above. In our Introduction we have already touched to relation Sonnet 88. Let it now be read studiously in relation with Sonnets 89 and 90. The author in Sonnet 89 says to the King:

SAY that thou didst forsake me for some fault,
And I will comment upon that offence;
Speak of my lameness, and I straight will halt,
Against thy reasons making no defence.
Thou canst not, love, disgrace me half so ill,
To set a form upon desired change,
As I'll myself disgrace: knowing thy will,
I will acquaintance strangle and look strange,
Be absent from thy walks, and in my tongue
Thy sweet beloved name no more shall dwell,
Lest I, too much profane, should do it wrong

And haply of our old acquaintance tell.
For thee against myself I'll vow debate,
For I must ne'er love him whom thou dost hate."

Being now forsaken by the King, the author in the foregoing asks him to say that it was for some fault, and that against his reasons, he will make no defence; that if it was for reform, or "To set a form upon desired change" he would outdo the King in disgracing himself, and says:

"For thee against myself I'll vow debate,
For I must ne'er love him whom thou dost hate."

That is, he must not love himself, being hated by the King. And he opens Sonnet 90 with:

THEN hate me when thou wilt; if ever, now;
Now, while the world is bent my deeds to cross,
Join with the spite of fortune, make me bow,
And do not drop in for an after-loss:
Ah, do not, when my heart hath 'scaped this sorrow,
Come in the rearward of a conquer'd woe;
Give not a windy night a rainy morrow,
To linger out a purposed overthrow.
If thou wilt leave me, do not leave me last,
When other petty griefs have done their spite,
But in the onset come; so shall I taste
At first the very worst of fortune's might,
And other strains of woe, which now seem woe,
Compared with loss of thee will not seem so."

At the mentioned interview, the King is said to have promised Bacon pardon upon his voluntary submission, if the Peers failed to recognize his merit, and convicted him. We understand the King's failure to do this, as agreed, to be the "thou art forsworn" of this Sonnet 88, and the "bed-vow broke" of Sonnet 152. As to this bed-rock vow, of pardon and its breach between King and counsel, see Bacon on the marriage between princes and their counselors.

In Sonnet 88, note its words, "That thou in losing me shalt win much glory." They show that the author was aware that his overthrow was to be an honor to the King. Into relation with them, we quote Bacon's letter to the King's favorite, Buckingham, the day following the sentence pronounced against him, thus: "My Very Good Lord: I hear yesterday was a day of very great honor to his Majesty, which I do congratulate. I hope, also, his Majesty may reap honor out of my adversity, as he hath done strength out of my prosperity. His Majesty knows best his own ways; and for me to despair of him, were a sin not to be forgiven. I thank God I have overcome the bitterness of this cup by Christian resolution, so that worldly matters are but mint and cumin. God ever preserve you." "Bacon's letters", vol. 7, p. 282.

Touching the "spite of fortune" upon the author, mentioned in Sonnet 90, last quoted, see, please, Sonnets 25, 29, 37 and 111. And were these in detail the experiences of William Shaksper with his sovereign? ha! We but call attention. We leave the reader to his reflection.

Concerning Bacon's mentioned interview with the King himself, see, please, Sonnet 113, which begins, "Since I left you;" and Sonnet 57 has, "When you have bid your servant once adieu." We understand the Sonnets here considered to indicate the very life of experience, and to have been couched by Bacon at, or near, the transit of events. Sonnet 113 shows the effect which the consent to abandon his defense had upon his mind. It is in these words:

>SINCE I left you, mine eye is in my mind;
>And that which governs me to go about
>Doth part his function and is partly blind,
>Seems seeing, but effectually is out;
>For it no form delivers to the heart
>Of bird, of flower, or shape, which it doth latch,
>Of his quick objects hath the mind no part,
>Nor his own vision holds what it doth catch;
>For if it see the rudest or gentlest sight,
>The most sweet favour or deformed'st creature,
>The mountain or the sea, the day or night,
>The crow or dove, it shapes them to your feature:
>>Incapable of more, replete with you,
>>My most true mind thus makes mine eye untrue."

Note its closing words "replete with you"—the King. See "you"—the King—also, in Sonnet 112. The referred to, as well as the quoted Sonnets, should be studied. Yes, Reader, studied.

Their numbering, let it be remembered, has nothing whatever to do with their subject-matter. It greatly confuses their true relations. They are hooded as already stated in four ways: by an Enigma, by an ante-date, by numbering, and by cover words. The cover words do not, however, concern this division of the Sonnets. As an egg will yield its meat only upon cracking the shell, so will these Sonnets only, upon their correct placing and interpretation.

Bacon's defense, had it been made, would have drawn much odium upon the King; and he evidently did not propose to have it made as we shall see later. Bacon ever taught that the crown should, from the King's own errors, be shielded, and this though at the sacrifice of any of his ministers. And the whole tenor of the Sonnets here referred to, shows that their author, whoever he was, was being submerged to shield the King; and as in Sonnet 125 to "render only me for thee." The author says:

> WERE'T aught to me I bore the canopy,
> With my extern the outward honouring,
> Or laid great bases for eternity,
> Which prove more short than waste or ruining?
> Have I not seen dwellers on form and favour
> Lose all, and more, by paying too much rent,
> For compound sweet forgoing simple savour,
> Pitiful thrivers, in their gazing spent?
> No, let me be obsequious in thy heart,
> And take thou my oblation, poor but free,
> Which is not mix'd with seconds, knows no art,
> But mutual render, only me for thee.
>   Hence, thou suborn'd informer! a true soul
>   When most impeach'd stands least in thy control."

Did space permit, we would gladly give Bacon's words concerning "seconds" here referred to. They will be touched later in Chapter 4 in connection with the plays. Touching the words of this Sonnet, "I bore the canopy, with my extern," we may say that the cry for reform, at the time, began concerning the exactions of Buckingham and his delinquents, and was totally abandoned as to all upon Bacon's submission. And Buckingham's advisor Williams stepped into Bacon's shoes as Chancellor of England. Later through Buckingham's influence, as we shall see, he stayed Bacon's pardon at the seal.

To secure this submission was, we judge, the King's motive for the interview with Bacon touched earlier. The evidence satisfies us that there were two interviews, one sought by the King, the other by Bacon. Bacon said to Buckingham at the outset: "I woo nobody. I do but listen."

As to the words of the Sonnet, "Or laid great bases for eternity," we need say nothing here. This concerns the author's philosophy, that "something new" of Sonnet 59 and its "tables" of Sonnet 122, which "tables"— see all of second book of "Novum Organum"—were to bear his name to future ages, and make him long outlive "that idle rank" which downed him. Bacon's entire system was based upon his "Tables of Discovery."

This, however, must be examined in connection with that particular division of the Sonnets which concerns philosophy. Then their author's great love for it, and his "love wooing of truth," will be shown.

Fear for the effect which their author's fall might have upon it, finds expression in Sonnet 107 where this great reflector of light refers to his fall, as an eclipse; and to himself, as the "mortal moon." He says in Sonnet 60 that the eclipse was a crooked one.

Let the reader now call the "compound sweet" of this Sonnet 125 into direct relation with the "eager compounds" of Sonnet 118, and the King's "ne'er-cloying sweetness." Note in it a portion of Bacon's nest of medical terms, applied ever by him to mental, as to material operations; and this, throughout the plays, as in his attributed work. This Sonnet 118 concerns disease and cure. It is designed to show that a healthful state was brought to medicine. Touching this in Sonnet 88 we have:

>"Upon thy part I can set down a story
>Of faults conceal'd, wherein I am attainted,
>That thou in losing me shalt win much glory."

The history of Bacon's fall shows that he did set down the story. He had no trial, but was convicted only upon a story or statement formulated by himself. How much there was in it to justify conviction, we leave to the reader. Spedding, in his Life of Bacon, Vol. 7, page 251, upon this point, says: "We are compelled to fall back upon Bacon himself, as being really our only authority; and to hold him guilty to the extent of his own confession, and no further." The King's "drugs," his "ne'er cloying sweetness," of which the author fell sick, in Sonnet 118, are said to be poison, and not medicine. We will give it later.

At the writing of Sonnet 49 his hypnotism upon the author began to fade. He says:

>AGAINST that time, if ever that time come,
>When I shall see thee frown on my defects,
>When as thy love hath cast his utmost sum,
>Call'd to that audit by advised respects;
>Against that time when thou shalt strangely pass
>And scarcely greet me with that sun, thine eye,
>When love, converted from the thing it was,
>Shall reasons find of settled gravity,—
>Against that time do I ensconce me here
>Within the knowledge of mine own desert,
>And this my hand against myself uprear,
>To guard the lawful reasons on thy part:
>>To leave poor me thou hast the strength of laws,
>>Since why to love I can allege no cause."

These are not our words, Reader. It is Francis Bacon's own story we are trying to let him tell. Let it be here noted that the King had cast upon the author his utmost sum of love; and that he by "advised respects" was called to his "audit."

Knight in his History of England, Vol. 3, p. 300, says: "The King had a loathsome way of lolling his arms about his favorites' necks, and kissing them."

This King had secret wiles as did his mother the Queen of Scots. What less than hypnotism can account for Sonnets 26, 112, 113, 114, 150 and others; whoever may have been their author. See here our "Defoe Period," p. 161, note 1. But a few months before, the King had raised Bacon to the desired title of Saint—St. Alban. Finding the King's will, Bacon now placed himself in the same attitude towards him that he placed Cranmer, towards the King, in the play of Henry the 8th, to be touched later in Chapter 4. Let the would-be doubting reader pause here for reflection. In a letter to Buckingham, the now King's right hand, following his fall Bacon says: "I am not guilty to myself of any unworthiness except perhaps too much softness at the beginning of my troubles." "Bacon's Letters," Vol. 7, p. 313. Note in the foregoing Sonnet Bacon's distinctive use of the words "against," and "advised respects."

As to the King's pretended sympathy and tears at the beginning of Bacon's troubles we quote his own words to the King upon being released from the Tower—he was there but two days—thus: "But your Majesty that did shed tears at the beginning of my troubles, will I hope shed the dew of your grace and goodness upon me in the end." "Bacon's Letters," Vol. 7, p. 281. As to these tears of the King which were to "ransom all ill deeds," see Sonnet 34. In Sonnet 35 which surely must be read, he tells him to grieve no more. But after his trifling and delay in pardoning Bacon, as agreed, his tears are in Sonnet 119 referred to, thus:

> WHAT potions have I drunk of Siren tears,
>   Distill'd from limbecks foul as hell within,
> Applying fears to hopes and hopes to fears,
> Still losing when I saw myself to win!
> What wretched errors hath my heart committed,
> Whilst it hath thought itself so blessed never!
> How have mine eyes out of their spheres been fitted
> In the distraction of this madding fever!
> O benefit of ill! now I find true
> That better is by evil still made better;
> And ruin'd love, when it is built anew,
> Grows fairer than at first, more strong, far greater.
>   So I return rebuked to my content
>   And gain by ill thrice more than I have spent."

Touching the "fears to hopes and hopes to fears" of this Sonnet, see Sonnet 107.

The King's bed-rock vow of pardon being now broken, Bacon in Sonnet 87 bids him "Farewell." In it he says: "And so my patent back again is swerving." Refers he here to his own lawful right to the crown? Let this Sonnet be called to relation with Sonnet 152 where the author tells the King that to enlighten him "he gave eyes to blindness." He reminds him here of his "bed-vow broke", touched earlier as to the marriage between Princes and their counsellors p. 32. He then says to him: "All my honest faith in thee is lost." And he closes it with:

> "For I have sworn thee fair; more perjured I,
>   To swear against the truth so foul a lie!"

Touching now his "too much softness," his desire to please, Bacon in Sonnet 147 says:

> MY love is as a fever, longing still
> For that which longer nurseth the disease,
> Feeding on that which doth preserve the ill,
> The uncertain sickly appetite to please.
> My reason, the physician to my love,
> Angry that his prescriptions are not kept,
> Hath left me, and I desperate now approve
> Desire is death, which physic did except.
> Past cure I am, now reason is past care,
> And frantic-mad with evermore unrest;
> My thoughts and my discourse as madmen's are,
> At random from the truth vainly express'd;
>> For I have sworn thee fair and thought thee bright,
>> Who art as black as hell, as dark as night."

Would the author, whoever he was, have ventured this Sonnet touching the King uncovered?—hence the ante-date, the Enigma, the numbering and the cover words.

Touching the expression, "Desire is death, which physic did except," in the Sonnet last quoted, we may say, that, upon reaching the Tower, Bacon at once wrote Buckingham, saying "Good My Lord: Procure the warrant for my discharge this day. Death, I thank God, is so far from being unwelcome to me as I have called for it (as Christian resolution would permit), any time these two months. But to die before the time of his Majesty's grace and in this disgraceful place, is even the worst that could be; and when I am dead, he is gone that was always in one tenor, a true and perfect servant to his Master and one that was never author of any immoderate, no, nor unsafe, no (I will say it) not unfortunate counsel." And he closes by saying that while for reformation sake the decision was proper "I was the justest Chancellor that hath been in the five changes since Sir Nicholas Bacon's time." "Bacon's Letters," Vol. 7, p. 280. See here Sonnet 71. As to the expression "which physic did except" in the foregoing Sonnet see p. 213, 241, and 329. Is there any other Englishman which these garments will fit, reader?

The appetite to please, in our last quoted Sonnet was the disease which brought to medicine the "healthful state" of Sonnet 118 where we have:

LIKE as, to make our appetites more keen,
With eager compounds we our palate urge,
As, to prevent our maladies unseen,
We sicken to shun sickness when we purge,
Even so, being full of your ne'er-cloying sweetness,
To bitter sauces did I frame my feeding
And, sick of welfare, found a kind of meetness
To be diseased ere that there was true needing.
Thus policy in love, to anticipate
The ills that were not, grew to faults assured
And brought to medicine a healthful state
Which, rank of goodness, would by ill be cured:
  But thence I learn, and find the lesson true,
  Drugs poison him that so fell sick of you."

That the author, whoever he was, was not "guilty to himself" of any unworthiness, see Sonnet 121. It will be given later in Chapter 4.

Sonnet 66 and one or two others concern the leach Buckingham who without law or justice filched from Bacon his York House, his valued early home. It is in these words:

> TIRED with all these, for restful death I cry,
>   As, to behold desert a beggar born,
> And needy nothing trimm'd in jollity,
> And purest faith unhappily forsworn,
> And gilded honour shamefully misplaced,
> And maiden virtue rudely strumpeted,
> And right perfection wrongfully disgraced,
> And strength by limping sway disabled,
> And art made tongue-tied by authority,
> And folly, doctor-like controlling skill,
> And simple truth miscall'd simplicity,
> And captive good attending captain ill;
>   Tired with all these, from these would I be gone,
>   Save that, to die, I leave my love alone."

"Love," as used in this Sonnet and in Sonnets 19, 29, 63, 64, 65, 76, 107 and others, refers to the author's philosophy, his felt mission, his Great Instauration already touched. "Love," in the Sonnets, concerns chiefly King, Queen or philosophy. The context must determine this. Philosophy is, at times, by poetic license, addressed as a person. See Sonnets 29, 37, 75, 78 and others. We find no unlawful love in the Sonnets, nor woman referred to, save Queen Elizabeth.

Returning to the Sonnet we would say, yes, Bacon had fallen. Had he also fallen among thieves? See in this "Bacon's Letters", Vol. 7, p. 310 to 334. See p. 313 and 314 as to his promised pardon by both King and Buckingham. Through the influence of Buckingham, Williams now stopped it at the seal, Buckingham giving Bacon to understand that York House must first be his. As to Buckingham's promise of pardon, to Bacon, of the whole sentence, we, p. 313, have Bacon's own words for it. He says: "As for that I find, your Lordship knoweth as well as I what promises you made me, and iterated them both by message and from your mouth, consisting of three things, the pardon of the whole sentence, some help for my debts, and an annual (pension) which your Lordship ever set at 2000£ as obtained, and 3000£ in hope." He then says: "I do not think any except a Turk or Tartar would wish to have another chop out of me." Having procured the abandonment of his defense, he was now in their trap. His friends advise him to make his words to Buckingham now all of "sweetmeats." He no longer had the King's ear, who said to Buckingham, "You played an after-game well." That "These blenches gave my heart another youth." See please Sonnets 110, 119, 123 and 68. From the paper touching the promises made him, p. 314, he says: "For me, if they judge by that which is past, they judge of the weather of this year by an almanack of the old year." See later "Bickerstaff and the almanack."

Bacon gives now the King warning in Sonnet 140, and says:

BE wise as thou art cruel; do not press
My tongue-tied patience with too much disdain;
Lest sorrow lend me words and words express
The manner of my pity-wanting pain.
If I might teach thee wit, better it were,
Though not to love, yet, love, to tell me so;
As testy sick men, when their deaths be near,
No news but health from their physicians know;
For if I should despair, I should grow mad,
And in my madness might speak ill of thee:
Now this ill-wresting world is grown so bad,

HIS SELF-TOLD OVERTHROW

Mad slanderers by mad ears believed be.
That I may not be so, nor thou belied,
Bear thine eyes straight, though thy proud heart go wide."

That Francis Bacon's overthrow was a covert piece of work is indicated by the "tongue-tied patience" of this, and of Sonnet 66. It appears later from Archbishop Tennison's words touching Bacon's troubles, who says: "The great cause of his suffering is to many a secret. I leave them to find it out by his words to King James. 'I wish that as I am the first, so I may be the last of sacrifices in your times; and when from private appetite it is resolved that a creature shall be sacrificed, it is easy to pick up sticks enough from any thicket, whither it hath strayed, to make a fire to offer it with.'"

Basil Montagu in his "Life and Works of Bacon," Vol. 1, p. 99, says: "The obligation to silence imposed upon Bacon, extended to his friends after he was in the grave."

Bribery was but the after-game, reader, brought forward when Bacon was securely within the trap. He was first charged with others as a Referee in a business which the King did not purpose to have opened. Bacon was preparing to meet this. It was totally abandoned, the bribery charges taking its place, as we shall see later in Chapter 4, in connection with the "several plot" of that subtle Sonnet 137. We would be gratified to know that this work of ours might one day become a plank in the platform of a society to be reared, to investigate Bacon's reform, and said Plot.

As to the "mad slanderers" touched in the Sonnet last quoted, see Sonnet 70. See also Bacon's own words to

Buckingham concerning them. "Bacon's Letters," Vol. 7, p. 296. He here likewise says: "I never took penny for releasing any thing I stopped at the seal, I never took penny for any commission or things of that nature, I never shared with any servant for any second or inferior profit. My offences I have myself recorded; wherein I studied, as a good confessant, guiltiness and not excuse; and therefore I hope it leaves me fair to the King's grace, and will turn many men's hearts to me."

These offences will be found set out at p. 252 to 261. Without claiming Bacon to be an angel, make now an example of corrupt bribery out of any one of these charges, you who can. They never would have been made, nor would they have prevailed, reader, had it not been for that which lay behind. The true causes involved in the overthrow, the rolling in the dirt of this chief pillar of Protestantism must yet be told, reader. His suave letters and speeches to those whom he well knew were seeking his ruin; and made while endeavoring to prevent the sequestration of his estate have greatly befogged it, as have undated, misplaced and garbled papers, as well as those purposely withheld or kept out of sight.

His critics agree that avarice was not his fault, but rather liberality. His great secret mission, his Posthumous Pocket labors evidently drew heavily, and had for years, upon his means. Even after his fall he speaks of "the good pens that forsake me not." The gratuities or gifts he received came freely from the well to do class; and to this time, when the reform set in, had been the custom of the Chancellors. This reform became now part of his great mission. From Sonnet 48 we judge little could be secured from the King, either in aid or protection of his

HIS SELF-TOLD OVERTHROW

literary work—his "jewels." See in this please our "Defoe Period," p. 222 to 225.

As Bacon would not, during his troubles, disclose his feelings to the public, so he talked them into the Sonnets here under review, leaving them thus to time. They may, in a sense, be regarded as soliloquies. Ever he was reminding himself by notes, as is well known. Sonnet 77 was one of these self reminders. Are not these Sonnets all the same concise talkers in verse, as is his concededly written Sonnet touching Queen Elizabeth given in Chapter I? See p. 18.

As Dante sang his sorrows in his "Divine Comedy," so did Bacon his in these Sonnets. We do not say they came to the King's eye, though some of them may have. In Sonnet 26 he says: "Till then not show my head where thou mayst prove me." Throughout, Bacon's writings show a distinctive emphasis upon duty and obedience. This emphasis upon duty should be noted in the mentioned Sonnet 26, and throughout the plays.

To the time of his fall he was a believer in the doctrine of passive obedience and the divine right of Kings. Following that event he began vigorously to retailor those doctrines. This will graphically appear in his Posthumous Pocket labors, as we shall see. When he said following his fall, "My story is proud," he but tamely expressed what he proclaimed in Sonnets 55 and 107. In Sonnet 55 he says his praise shall find room "Even in the eyes of all posterity;" and he says Sonnet 107 will be his monument "when tombs of brass are spent." Are these Sonnets interpreted, Reader? If words mean anything, do not Sonnets 88, 89 and 90 portray the overthrow of their author, whoever he may have been?

Returning now to Sonnet 57, given at the opening of this Chapter, we invite careful thought to its words:

"Whilst I, my sovereign, watch the clock for you,
Nor think the bitterness of absence sour
When you have bid your servant once adieu."

Are we justified in saying the author, whoever he was, here refers to his King as Sovereign, and himself as subject? As to watching the clock for him, we quote Bacon thus:

"For the star-chamber business I shall (as you write) keep the clock on going, which is hard to do when sometimes the wheels are too many and sometimes too few."

As to that distinctive expression, "the bitterness of absence sour," Bacon says: "There be (saith the Scriptures) that turn judgment into wormwood, and surely there be also that turn it into vinegar; for injustice maketh it bitter and delays make it sour."

But such proofs; and proofs as to language features, can not all be handled in one short work designed to outline the field for research, and they must come later. It seems proper, however, to say here, that the vocabulary of the Plays and Sonnets furnishes the highest possible point in the proofs of Bacon's authorship. While able to throw his composition into almost any form, and so carry it, he was still unable to conceal his wonderful vocabulary. Could the untutored Shaksper have possessed identity of vocabulary with the cultured Bacon? Bacon used but one class of words, and these follow ever the line of physics, and never metaphysics. He applied the same words to mind that he did to matter or material things. He himself says: "Be not troubled about metaphysics. When true physics have been discovered, there will be no metaphysics. Beyond the true physics is divinity only."

He, in tabular methods stayed and fed ever, on external nature, God's works; and never like Aristotle spun theories, or made words, from that evolved from human ideation. He never theorized about what is in mind, but was ever attentive to the forms or shows of motives. He labored in the wilderness, and the plays were his woodnotes. He was, indeed, the marvel of the ages. In vocabulary, having once placed a word, that was ever his word for that place. He used not synonyms for it. In this, he never had an equal. This was why, in Sonnet 76, "every word doth almost tell my name." For the reasons stated, he was the most objective of all writers, and this applies to the Plays and Sonnets, as to his attributed work. As in the Plays, he stands behind an assumed, a hyphened name, so in the Sonnets he stands behind an Enigma and an assumed date; and both name and date are but shields, and have stood now as masks, nearly three hundred years. Francis Bacon no longer needs these shields, nor should they longer befog the intellect. As these title-pages are their author's own choice, so should they, we think, remain unchanged.

CHAPTER III

FRANCIS BACON'S WONDER. HIS TABULAR SYSTEM OF PHILOSOPHY. THAT SOMETHING ABSOLUTELY NEW OF THE SHAKESPEARE SONNET 59 AND ITS ETERNIZED "TABLES" OF SONNET 122 AND ITS "GREAT BASES FOR ETERNITY" OF SONNETS 124 AND 125; IN OTHER WORDS, HIS "NOBLEST BIRTH OF TIME," HIS "NEW BORN CHILD."

WE are to say something new to the reader in this chapter, concerning the Baconian philosophy, which its critics, have thus far failed to discover; as well as to unite that philosophy with those of his Shakespeare Sonnets which concern it. We will endeavor to open to the student, as well as to interest the general reader. We trust the Baconian student will nowhere else find so concise an outline of the vital parts of the Baconian method. This anatomy should reward any labor he may bestow upon this work.

In earlier pages we have touched to relation the chief of those Sonnets which concern the fall of their author, whoever he may have been.

We would here call to relation the chief of those which concern that wonder, his tabular system of philosophy; and its eternized tables. For ease in apprehending the philosophy touched upon in the Sonnets to be reviewed, it seems proper at the outset to premise certain central thoughts concerning it.

The Baconian system was in method absolutely new. It was based on distinctive "Tables of Discovery." They

HIS COMPOSED WONDER

are important in that all else in the system is based upon them. All other systems of philosophy are logical systems, and based on arguments.

This philosophy, though, we are the first to lay the claim, took origin in Bacon's investigation of the subject of light; which he calls "God's first creature." In his subtle doctrine of forms, light is God's first form or law.

The wonder of the system arose out of disclosures which its tables revealed to him, to wit, the forms or laws of what he calls "the simple natures;" as heat, cold, rare, dense, fluid, solid, light, heavy, etc.

Referring to these "simple natures," Bacon says: "And the truth is that the knowledge of simple natures well examined and defined is as light; it gives entrance to all the secrets of nature's workshop, and virtually includes and draws after it whole bands and troops of works, and opens to us the sources of the noblest axioms; and yet in itself it is of no great use. So also the letters of the alphabet in themselves and apart have no use or meaning, yet they are the subject matter, for the composition and apparatus of all discourse."

His great "Alphabet of Nature," his, as yet, undisclosed doctrine of forms starts here, Reader. Made he letters of the alphabet, or selected ancient fables, represent these "simple natures?" And what about the "sacred ceremonies" or Hebrew mysteries? See our "Defoe Period," p. 75. He elsewhere calls these "simple natures," "surds." He calls them "forms." See Aph. 7, book 2, of the "New Organ." Yet he says: "Forms are but fictions of the human mind, unless you call the laws of action by that name." He says: "The form of light is the law of light," "the form of heat is the law of heat," and so of the other "simple natures," which he says are few, and as an alphabet. While these "simple natures" or forms can be revealed only by means of his "Tables of Discovery"—now to our point—he nowhere in his writings tells how to find any one of them. This was by design. This was reserved to his Interpreter and to posterity as we will show later from his own words. Had he disclosed how to find the forms or laws of the "simple natures," this would have disclosed his "Alphabet of Nature," and so untimely have revealed his Posthumous Pocket labors. These thoughts are new, Reader, and if right they show Bacon's new system of induction to have been unfairly criticised, without having it. This will appear later.

Its "Tables of Discovery" were to be structured from selected particulars of knowledge drawn from a Natural History framed after his own peculiar method, and this History, was itself to be the first stage of selection.

Of the two books of his crowning work the "Novum Organum," in English words—"New Organ"—the first was designed chiefly to purge and prepare the mind for the reception of the new method.

The second book was designed to teach how from ordinary and "Prerogative Instances," to structure the "Tables of Discovery" alluded to in the Sonnets to be reviewed.

The structure, of the tables, however, was one thing. To teach how properly to make use of them, quite another. These standing tables, when structured, were their author's "Places of Invention." The deer is sooner caught within the enclosure of tables, than in the forest at large, of Natural History. They hold and frame the mental energies to the sought region of discovery.

To show now how to make use of these "Tables of Discovery," and the disclosures made by them, constitutes the true Key to the system. This Key, let it be remembered Bacon called his "Formula of Interpretation." This "Formula" was to minister to the reason.

The Natural History was to minister to the sense; the "Tables of Discovery" were to minister to the memory; and this "Formula of Interpretation," by means of an "Ascending and Descending Scale of Axioms," was to unfold, in use, the wonder of Bacon's inductive method.

Touching this third ministration, that is, to the reason, Bacon says: "Therefore in the third place we must use Induction, true and legitimate induction, which is the very Key of Interpretation."

This Key, the "Formula," when placed, should enter the "New Organ" at Aphorism 21 of its second book. This it was, which was to be handed on with selection and care to posterity undisclosed. This will distinctly appear as well in his open, as in his Cypher work.

By design, this "Formula," this new light, was never placed in the Lamp, the "New Organ," as we shall see. It was structured as was the "New Organ" itself, for the use of an Interpreter. See the closing paragraph of its second book. For detailed instructions now to his Interpreter, see Basil Montagu's "Life of Bacon," Vol. 2, p. 543 to 551. We do not find it in Speddings' works. From these instructions we quote briefly thus:

"Let him who comes to interpret thus prepare and qualify himself; let him not be a follower of novelty, nor of custom or antiquity; neither let him embrace the license of contradicting or the servitude of authority. Let him not be hasty to affirm or unrestrained in doubting, but let him produce everything marked with a certain degree of probation. Let hope be the cause of labor to him, not of idleness. Let him estimate things not by their rareness, difficulty, or credit, but by their real importance. Let him manage his private affairs under a mask, yet with some regard for the provisions of things."

We here emphasize to the reader, that Bacon's system of philosophy was never intended, by him, to subvert or take the place of existing methods. In Aph. 128 of his "New Organ," book 1, he says: "I frankly declare that what I am introducing will be but little fitted for such purposes as these, since it cannot be brought down to common apprehension, save by effects and works only."

It was to be carried forward covertly under a secret guidance and control. Its discoveries were from thence to be radiated upon society. Later we shall claim to the reader that the mentioned "Formula of Interpretation" was from the outset the true wonder of the Baconian system; and that it was never revealed by Bacon, at least, while living.

This tabular method was, we judge, early in use by him, and for a considerable time prior to his attempt to apply it to philosophy. We judge the "New Organ" was but an attempt to perfect and systematize a method which Bacon, as to "the simple natures," had already called into use. In a letter to the King, at its publication in October 1620, he says: "There be two of your council and one other bishop of this land that know I have been about some such work near thirty years; so I made no haste."

To indicate the use of this method in his Shakespeare plays, as well as in philosophy, we quote the opening words of Aph. 127 of his "New Organ," book I, thus: "It may also be asked (in the way of doubt rather than objection) whether I speak of natural philosophy only, or whether I mean that the other sciences, logic, ethics, and politics, should be carried on by this method. Now I certainly mean what I have said to be understood of them all; and as the common logic, which governs by the syllogism, extends not only to natural but to all sciences; so does mine also, which proceeds by induction, embrace everything. For I form a history and tables of discovery for anger, fear, shame, and the like; for matters political; and again for the mental operations of memory, composition and division, judgment and the rest; not less than for heat and cold, or light, or vegetation, or the like." Touching "characters" in the plays, see Bacon's "Phil. Works" by Spedding, Vol. 5, p. 20 to 31; and Vol. 4, p. 456 to 476.

Concerning philosophy, in connection with the theatre, Bacon says: "For we regard all the systems of philosophy hitherto received or imagined, as so many plays brought out and performed, creating fictitious and theatrical worlds."

His own philosophy he first outlined in a work which he entitled, "The Noblest Birth of Time." This birth was in his Hamlet "the great baby" yet in its swaddlings and was by Bacon's own hand recast or reswaddled, twelve different times before its publication in 1620, as the "New Organ." It was then out of its swaddlings, and was by Bacon called, "my new born child," as we shall see. He presented a copy of it to his literary friend Mathews, saying: "I have now at last taught that child to go, at the swaddling whereof you were." "Bacon's Letters," Vol. 3, p. 256. This undated letter was misplaced by Spedding.

The purpose of foisting "the great baby" into this play—it is not later referred to—was but a touch to indicate the reform intended. This babe was to tell of the actors, the players, through whom it was to be introduced.

They are said to be brief abstracts; or chronicles of the time, and the time is said to be out of joint.

Do "the brief abstracts," allude to the "tables?" The tables are twice distinctly referred to in Act I. Sc. 5. They minister to the memory, as we have seen. In Act 2, Sc. 2, Hamlet says to Ophelia: "Thine evermore, most dear lady, whilst this machine is to him, Hamlet."

To what "machine," please, can Hamlet here allude?

When our critic shall have exhausted the wonder of his wit in vain to determine, we come thus to his relief.

In many places in his writings Bacon calls his new method a "machine," his "new logical machine." In a letter to the King concerning it, he says: "I have constructed the machine but the stuff must be gathered from the facts of nature."

Let, now, the foregoing be considered by the reader, but as a brief side-light to this our second vintage on the so called Shakespeare Sonnets.

We would emphasize to him at the outset, that the author of the Sonnets, whoever he was, had produced or invented something rare, something absolutely new; which he calls "a composed wonder"—a child. It was surely new, unless the author's brains were beguiled, in which case only, it was but a second birth, or "burden."

To make this point sure to the reader, we quote Sonnet 59. Its author—was it Shaksper?—says:

IF there be nothing new, but that which is
Hath been before, how are our brains beguiled,
Which, labouring for invention, bear amiss
The second burden of a former child!
O, that record could with a backward look,
Even of five hundred courses of the sun,

Show me your image in some antique book,
Since mind at first in character was done!
That I might see what the old world could say
To this composed wonder of your frame;
Whether we are mended, or whether better they,
Or whether revolution be the same.
  O, sure I am, the wits of former days
  To subjects worse have given admiring praise."

In this Sonnet, and throughout the plays, note Bacon's distinctive words "invention," "image," "characters," "frame," "mended," "revolution," "wits," and his oft used expression, "sure I am." To instance in the word "image." Bacon says: "Knowledge is the image of existence." He says: "Words are but images of thoughts." He says: "For all color is the broken image of light." In the plays we have, "the image of authority," "the image of power," "the image of my cause." Note in this Sonnet and in Sonnets 38, 76, 103, and 105, Bacon's ever used word "invention" to indicate mental operations. See here please, our "Defoe Period," p. 135. Brevity must, however, restrain our hand from the language features. We here but outline our claim.

The foregoing Sonnet begins by saying that the author's brains are beguiled, if there be not something new, something before unknown; and later referred to as "a composed wonder;" and indicates a desire that when 500 years have elapsed, he, the author, might know what the world could say of it; and whether he, or "they,"—the ancients—were best. Shaksper? ha!

In the "five hundred courses of the sun" may be noted Bacon's distinctive claim that the sun and heavens move around the earth as a center, contrary to the accepted opinion of astronomers.

Should the reader prefer now his prejudices to his intelligence, and so avoid belief, he had best read no farther.

Into relation with this child—"the composed wonder" —of the Sonnet, under review, we introduce Francis Bacon's letter to the University of Cambridge, on presenting to it a copy of his "New Organ," thus:

"As your son and pupil, I desire to lay in your bosom my new-born child. Otherwise I should hold it for a thing exposed. Let it not trouble you that the way is new; for in the revolutions of time such things must needs be. Nevertheless the ancients retain their proper honor—that is, of wit and understanding; for faith is due only to the Word of God and to experience. Now to bring the sciences back to experience is not permitted; but to grow them anew out of experience, though laborious, is practicable. May God bless you and your studies. Your most loving son." "Bacon's Letters" by Spedding Vol. 7, p. 136.

The foregoing Sonnet in its every detail falls into full relation with this letter, item by item.

As to its alluded to ancients, Bacon says: "Nay it doth more fully lay open that the question between me and the ancients is not of the virtue of the race, but of the rightness of the way." "Bacon's Letters" Vol. 4, p. 137. He says: "They knew little antiquity; they knew, except fable, not much above five hundred years before themselves."

As to the "second burden" of the Sonnet, we quote him thus: "It may be thought again that I am but doing what has been done before;—that the ancients themselves took the same course which I am now taking; and that it is likely therefore that I too; after all this stir and striving, shall come at last to some one of those systems which prevailed in ancient times." "New Organ" Aph. 125, book 1.

We may thus see that Francis Bacon regarded his method as absolutely new and unknown to the ancients, and in no sense a second birth or burden. To trace its origin in Bacon's mind read attentively his "Cupid and Caelum." "Phil. Works," Vol. 5, p. 461 to 500, and Vol. 3, p. 65 to 118. "Composed wonder!" Time has failed to yield a written scrap, of Sonnet, Play, or composed line, from Shaksper's pen, reader!

The wonder spoken of in the Sonnet is said to be, "this composed wonder of your frame"—nature.

Is not this in identity what Bacon claimed his "New Organ" to be?

By means of its "Tables of Discovery" it was to focalize and reveal the very frame of nature. This Aladdin's Lamp,—this search light—turned upon his "Natural History"—all nature—was to reveal the true doctrine of forms,—the forms of "the simple natures," and from thence, as we shall see, his great "Alphabet of Nature."

Touching forms Bacon says: "To God, truly, the Giver and Architect of Forms, and it may be to the angels and higher intelligences it belongs to have an affirmative knowledge of forms immediately, and from the first contemplation. But this assuredly is more than man can do, to whom it is granted only to proceed at first by negatives, and at last to end in affirmatives, after exclusion has been exhausted." "New Organ" Aph. 15, book 2.

Again, in presenting a copy of the "New Organ" to the King, Bacon, as to the things of which it treats, says: "Certainly they are quite new; totally new in their very kind; and yet they are copied from a very ancient model; even the world itself and the nature of things and of the mind. And to say truth, I am wont for my own part to regard this work as a child of time rather than of wit; the only wonder being that the first notion of the thing, and such great suspicions concerning matters long established, should have come into any man's mind. All the rest follows readily enough. And no doubt there is something of accident (as we call it) and luck as well in what men think as in what they do or say. But for this accident which I speak of, I wish that if there be any good in what I have to offer, it may be ascribed to the infinite mercy and goodness of God, and to the felicity of your Majesty's times; to which as I have been an honest and affectionate servant in my life, so after my death I may yet perhaps, through the kindling of this new light in the darkness of philosophy, be the means of making this age famous to posterity; and surely to the times of the wisest and most learned of Kings belongs of right the regeneration and restoration of the sciences." "Phil. Works," Vol. 4, p. 11.

Bacon's authorship of the Sonnet under review can surely require no further proof than its critical contrast by the reader, with his words here given. Note in this letter to the King the mentioned rare "wonder." Note that it is called a child; that it is totally new; that it was copied after the world as a model, or frame.

"Frame" as applied to nature in the Sonnet is Bacon's use. He says: "It is certain that of all powers in nature heat is the chief both in the frame of nature and in the works of art." As to the emphasis touching nature, we in Sonnet 127, have, "each hand hath put on nature's power." Bacon says: "Heat and cold are nature's two hands."

In a further letter to the King touching the "New Organ," "Bacon's Letters," Vol. 7, p. 120, he says: "This work is but a new body of clay, whereinto your Majesty by your countenance and protection, may breath life. And to tell your Majesty truly what I think, I account your favour may be to this work as much as an hundred years' time: for I am persuaded the work will gain upon men's minds in ages, but your gracing it may make it take hold more swiftly; which I would be glad of, it being a work meant not for praise or glory, but for practice, and the good of men. One thing, I confess, I am ambitious of, with hope, which is, that after these beginnings, and the wheel once set on going, men shall suck more truth out of Christian pens, than hitherto they have done out of heathen."

These purposes and doings were his, but a few months prior to his overthrow. This child was his Miranda, which he sought to wed to power. "Defoe Period," p. 319 to 346.

But this "new born child" of his letter is touched again in Sonnet 21, where the author says he does not seek to make a "proud compare" of his fair—his child—with others. He merely seeks truth in his description.

What, Reader, was the "child" of Sonnet 124, if not the child of philosophy?

It is in these words:

IF my dear love were but the child of state,
  It might for Fortune's bastard be unfather'd,
As subject to Time's love or to Time's hate,
Weeds among weeds, or flowers with flowers gather'd.
No, it was builded far from accident;
It suffers not in smiling pomp, nor falls
Under the blow of thralled discontent,
Whereto the inviting time our fashion calls:

> It fears not policy, that heretic,
> Which works on leases of short-number'd hours,
> But all alone stands hugely politic,
> That it nor grows with heat nor drowns with showers.
>> To this I witness call the fools of time,
>> Which die for goodness, who have lived for crime."

This "thralled discontent," this political unrest, this cry for reform, was touched into relation in Chapter 2.

The author here calls "the fools of time"—his detractors—to witness that his philosophy, his "dear love" was "builded far from accident," and that it falls not "under the blow of thralled discontent." True love he describes in Sonnet 116. In Sonnet 129 he tells of lust and its effects. In Sonnet 115, love, like philosophy, is said to be a babe in growth. In the plays he shows how, by lust, Kings, Kingdoms, and great persons are brought to their ruin.

As to the love-wooing of philosophy or truth, Bacon in his "Essay on Truth," says: "Yet truth which only doth judge itself, teacheth that the inquiry of truth which is the love-making or wooing of it, the knowledge of truth, which is the presence of it, and the belief of truth, which is the enjoying of it, is the sovereign good of human nature."

The author of the Sonnets subsequent to his fall centered his heart, his life, his "dear love" upon "thee" his child of philosophy, as may be clearly seen in Sonnet 37, where we have:

> AS a decrepit father takes delight
> To see his active child do deeds of youth,
> So I, made lame by fortune's dearest spite,
> Take all my comfort of thy worth and truth.
> For whether beauty, birth, or wealth, or wit,

Or any of these all, or all, or more,
Entitled in thy parts do crowned sit,
I make my love engrafted to this store:
So then I am not lame, poor, nor despised,
Whilst that this shadow doth such substance give
That I in thy abundance am sufficed
And by a part of all thy glory live.
   Look, what is best, that best I wish in thee;
   This wish I have; then ten times happy me!"

Let "unfather'd" in the previously quoted; and "decrepit father," in this Sonnet, be called to relation with their author's fall. Note Bacon's use of the words "shadow," and "substance," in this, in Sonnet 53, and throughout his attributed writings.

Again, "Haply, I think on thee," see Sonnet 29.

As to the distinctive use of the word "lame," in the previously quoted Sonnet we quote Bacon thus: "For (gracious Sovereign) if still, when the waters are stirred, another shall be set before me, your Majesty had need work a miracle, or else I shall be still a lame man to do your service."

Upon the publication of his "New Organ" in October 1620, criticism at once began at Rome, as elsewhere, concerning it. His great rival, Coke, said: "It is fit only for a ship of fools." The King said: "It is like the peace of God, it passeth all understanding." And what became of Father Redemptus Baranzano's letter to Bacon concerning it? See "Bacon's Letters," Vol. 7, p. 374 to 380, and 367 to 370. Had Bacon later a right to say to his literary friend Toby Mathews "And thou too O Brutus?" What motive lay behind his extensive garbling of Bacon's letters to him, blurring in them both names of persons and events which they concern?   This will be touched later in Chapter 4.

After Bacon had endured his eclipse—his fall—see what he says in Sonnet 107.

Having now touched to relation the "New Organ," as a whole, in Sonnet 59, and others, we here turn to its "tables" in Sonnet 122, where we have:

> THY gift, thy tables, are within my brain
>   Full character'd with lasting memory,
> Which shall above that idle rank remain
> Beyond all date, even to eternity;
> Or at the least, so long as brain and heart
> Have faculty by nature to subsist;
> Till each to razed oblivion yield his part
> Of thee, thy record never can be miss'd.
> That poor retention could not so much hold,
> Nor need I tallies thy dear love to score;
> Therefore to give them from me was I bold,
> To trust those tables that receive thee more:
>   To keep an adjunct to remember thee
>   Were to import forgetfulness in me."

As already stated, Bacon believed that only God, or possibly the higher intelligences, could have a knowledge of forms without aid of "Tables of Discovery." Does he mean to intimate that he may have this gift, in the foregoing Sonnet, and in the following? He says: "For Plato casteth his burden [see "second burden" in our quoted Sonnet 59] and saith *that he will revere him as a God, that can truly divide and define*; which cannot be but by true forms and differences. Wherein I join hands with him, confessing as much, as yet, assuming to myself little; for if any man can by the strength of his *anticipations* find out forms, I will magnify him with the foremost. But as any of them would say that if divers things which many men know by instruction and observation another knew by revelation and without those means, they would take him for somewhat supernatural and divine; so I do acknowledge that if any man can by anticipations reach to that which a weak and inferior wit may attain to by interpretation, he cannot receive too high a title." "Phil. Works," Vol. 3, p. 239.

Note "as yet assuming to myself little."

The "Tables of Discovery," as already stated, were to minister to the memory. And so, the author in the Sonnet under review, says the "tables are within my brain;" that they are "full character'd with lasting memory;" that his poor retention could not hold them; and therefore he was bold to give them forth. He says until both brain and heart, as well as the "tables,"—note "till each" have yielded their part of him; his record never can be missed. He says he does not need "tallies"—tables—to score the love of the giver of them.

And was it Shaksper whose name was to be distinguished and eternized by "tables?" and if Shaksper, what tables?

The author says they place him "above that idle rank"—those who had sought his ruin. Their enmity is directly alluded to in Sonnet 55, wherein the author likewise says his record shall live until a true judgment of himself is made. He says:

NOT marble, nor the gilded monuments
  Of princes, shall outlive this powerful rhyme;
But you shall shine more bright in these contents
Than unswept stone besmear'd with sluttish time.

> When wasteful war shall statues overturn,
> And broils root out the work of masonry,
> Nor Mars his sword nor war's quick fire shall burn
> The living record of your memory.
> 'Gainst death and all-oblivious enmity
> Shall you pace forth; your praise shall still find room
> Even in the eyes of all posterity
> That wear this world out to the ending doom.
>   So, till the judgment that yourself arise,
>   You live in this, and dwell in lovers' eyes."

The words "you," "your," "yourself," in this Sonnet are cover words wherein the author alludes to himself, as will appear from our 7th Division of the Sonnets.

Are not the last two Sonnets in direct line with the words of Sir Francis Bacon who says: "I have raised up a light in the obscurity of philosophy which will be seen centuries after I am dead."

For the benefit of those not familiar with Bacon's philosophic writings, we would say, that his system, his Great Instauration, was outlined in six parts. As but four of them were developed, these only need be considered by the student.

His "Advancement of Learning," was subsequent to his fall, recast and enlarged and was published in 1623 as the "De Augmentis," and as such, was made the 1st part of the Instauration. The "New Organ" was the 2nd part. His "Natural History" was the 3rd. The 4th part was his method of operating the "Tables of Discovery" by aid of the mentioned "Formula" or Key; which was for the use of an Interpreter, as already stated. In the closing paragraph itself of the "New Organ" we have "The rest need not be inquired into till we come to make Tables of Presentation for the work of the Interpreter concerning some particular nature." To find the "simple natures" he must first have "the Formula," the Key.

To show now that the whole system was subservient to the "Tables of Discovery" we quote from Aph. 92 of the "New Organ," book 1, thus: "And though the strongest means of inspiring hope will be to bring men to particulars; especially to particulars digested and arranged in my Tables of Discovery (the subject partly of the second, but much more of the fourth part of my Instauration) since this is not merely the promise of the thing but the thing itself."

Had Mr. Spedding called the mentioned Key or "Formula of Interpretation" into relation with Chapters 1 and 2 of book 6 of the "De Augmentis," which chapters concern the "Handing on of the Lamp or Method of Delivery to Posterity;" this would have placed the Baconian system in its true light, by informing the critics that the Interpreter of the "New Organ" and "the sons of science" must first have the "Formula;" which should enter its second book at Aph. 21; and which concerns the "Ascending and Descending scale of Axioms," or the disclosures, in the use, of the "Tables of Discovery."

To show now that the "Formula of Interpretation" which was to be reserved from publication was the very key to Bacon's new inductive method we quote him thus: "Now the popular induction (from which the proofs of principles themselves are attempted) is but a puerile toy, concluding at random, and perpetually in risk of being exploded by contradictory instances: insomuch that the dialecticians seem never once to have thought of the subject in earnest, turning from it in a sort of disdain, and hurrying on to other things. Meantime this is manifest, that the conclusions which are attained by any species of induction are at once both discovered and attested, and do not depend on axioms and middle truths, but stand on their own weight of evidence, and require no extrinsic proof. Much more then is it necessary that those axioms which are raised according to the true form of induction, should be of self-contained proof, surer and more solid than what are termed principles themselves; and this kind of induction is what we have been wont to term the formula of interpretation." Basil Montagu's "Life of Bacon," Vol. 2, p. 555.

To show now that Sir Francis Bacon intended to reserve this Key or "Formula of Interpretation" from the public to a private succession, we from an article concerning the publication of his writings entitled, "The Interpretation of Nature" quote thus:

"Now for my plan of publication—those parts of the work which have it for their object to find out and bring into correspondence such minds as are prepared and disposed for the argument, and to purge the floors of men's understandings, I wish to be published to the world and circulate from mouth to mouth, the rest I would have passed from hand to hand, with selection and judgment. Not but I know that it is an old trick of impostors to keep a few of their follies back from the public which are indeed no better than those they put forward: but in this case it is no imposture at all, but a sober foresight, which tells me that the formula itself of interpretation and the discoveries made by the same, will thrive better if committed to the charge of some fit and selected minds and kept private." "Bacon's Letters," Vol. 3, p. 87. Should the reader have a doubt here see Bacon's "Phil. Works," by Spedding, Vol. 1, p. 107 to 113.

It is thus manifest from Francis Bacon's own words, that this "Formula," the Key to his new method, which, as we have seen, was to minister to the reason, was to remain unpublished in the hands of a select few. We say, with the "Sons of Science" of his "New Atlantis."

The failure to recognize the significance of this Key or "Formula," to the system, and the misdating and misplacing the papers, which concern it, have confused and belittled the entire system. Its critics have thus pronounced upon a new system of philosophy with its wonder, its head-light, in abeyance. And so we have "Bacon did not know." "Bacon did not comprehend." "Bacon did not realize."

Mr. Spedding placed this undated paper as if written in 1603. See please his reasons, or rather his want of reasons for so placing it. Would one prepare for the general publication of his writings before producing them?

Like the "De Augmentis" it was translated into Latin, not done with his early works. It may have been originally designed as an introduction to it, or to the "New Organ." It has all of the ear-marks of having been written subsequent to the "New Organ." It concerns the publication of Bacon's writings to posterity. The part quoted will be found in the already mentioned article giving instructions to his Interpreter. There, as in the "New Atlantis," the Interpreter is called "my son," and the "Formula" is referred to thus: "One bright and radiant light of truth, my son, must be placed in the midst, which may illuminate the whole, and in a moment dispel all error." In the "New Atlantis," Bacon says: "God bless thee my son; I give thee the greatest jewel I have," referring thus to the basis of his new system. To this "jewel" we shall later have occasion to refer when we reach Sonnet 65.

As stated, to find and use the "simple natures" was the business of the "Formula" or Key. We are here at the point in the Baconian system where "Indirection must find direction out."

To discover now the law or form of "a simple nature" as of light, was by Bacon called "The freeing of a direction," to find it, as will appear in Aph. 4 and 10 of book 2 of the "New Organ."

"The freeing of a direction" to find the form! We are here at the threshold of Bacon's Wonder, his new induction; his "Noblest Birth of Time." This was the setting up of his "mark of knowledge," by the placing of "the white." "Phil. Works," Vol. 4, p. 126.

Neither in the "New Organ," nor in any place in Bacon's writings does he give a single example or attempt to describe this process—"the freeing of a direction"—to find the form of a "simple nature" save in one of the mentioned misplaced fragments known as "Valerius Terminus, or The Interpretation of Nature." He here distinctly informs the reader, however, that he does not purpose to reveal his method. By misplacing this paper his critics have concluded that he abandoned his intention. It has no date. Mr. Spedding has placed it as if written before 1605. See his reasons, or want of reasons, for so placing it. "Phil. Works," Vol. 3, p. 201 to 213. The wonders of the "Formula" are referred to at p. 247. The paper itself opens at p. 217.

On page 236, Bacon is investigating the subject of light and colors, and notably "the freeing of a direction" leading to the form of light. He here distinctly informs the reader that he does not intend to reveal his method. He says: "Now are you freed from air, but still you are tied to transparent bodies. To ascend further by scale I do forbear, partly because it would draw on the example to an over great length, but chiefly because it would open that which in this work I determine to reserve; for to pass through the whole history and observation of colors and objects visible were too long a digression; and our purpose is now to give an example of a free direction, thereby to distinguish and describe it; and not to set down a form of interpretation how to recover and attain it. But as we intend not now to reveal so we are circumspect not to mislead; and therefore (this warning being given) returning to our purpose in hand, we admit the sixth direction to be that all bodies or parts of bodies which are unequal equally, that is in a simple proportion, do represent whiteness; we will explain this, though we induce it not. It is then to be understood, that absolute equality produceth transparence, inequality in simple order or proportion produceth whiteness, inequality in compound or respective order or proportion produceth all other colors, and absolute or orderless inequality produceth blackness; which diversity, if so gross a demonstration be needful, may be signified by four tables; a blank, a chequer, a fret, and a medley; whereof the fret is evident to admit great variety."

The foregoing is but a more extended view of the subject but touched in the "New Organ" in Aph. 22 and 23 of book 2. And see "Phil. Works," Vol. 4, p. 361. Note here the subject of "inequality." Bacon says: "For such orderly inequality is in truth the daughter of the heavens and mother of generation." That the discovery of the configuration of bodies is as new a thing as the discovery of forms; and taught by an absolutely new method. See Aph. 7, 8 and 9 of book 2 of the "New Organ."

Thus from his own words may we see that Francis Bacon did not intend to disclose how to obtain a knowledge of the laws or forms of "the simple natures." That there may be now no escape from this conclusion, see please "Phil Works," Vol. 4, p. 29 and 262; and Vol. 5, p. 135.

This was to be supplied to the "New Organ" at Aph. 21 of book 2, by the reserved "Formula of Interpretation," as already stated.

In the prior Aph. 20, it should be noted, that trials to interpret by means of the tabular examples given, were; not to be by the "Formula," but by what Bacon calls the mere "Indulgence of the Understanding." These points we present for the benefit of the student of the system.

The "Tables of Discovery" should not be thought merely to reveal "forms." They are their author's places of invention. They unfold, as well, knowledge of "the configuration of bodies," and scintillate generally with information. Their business is to investigate the concrete to learn its disclosures—the abstract. The concrete is ever but the vehicle of the form. The laws of nature are all unseen. These tables are the "children" of Sonnet 77 which "nursed" take a new acquaintance of the mind.

The "simple natures" are forms of the 1st class and so concern Metaphysics and the Alphabet. Forms of the 2nd class are compound forms and concern Physics only. See Aph. 7, 8 and 9, of book 2 of the "New Organ." With those of the 1st class are we concerned in this work. When found they ease the opening of the 2nd class.

Never, for a moment, from the issue of his "Noblest Birth of Time" does Bacon appear to have lost faith in his method. He informs the reader, however, in many places in his writings, that there are no common grounds upon which to contrast his tabular method with those extant. And he says: "Even to deliver and explain what I bring forward is no easy matter; for things in themselves new will yet be apprehended with reference to the old."

Both Mr. Spedding and Mr. Ellis have so apprehended it. Mr. Ellis says: "For that his method is impracticable cannot I think be denied, if we reflect not only that it never has produced any result, but also that the process by which scientific truths have been established cannot be so presented as even to appear to be in accordance with it." "Phil. Works" Vol. 1, p. 38.

Mr. Spedding, same work, Vol. 3, p. 171, says: "His peculiar system of philosophy,—that is to say, the peculiar method of investigation, the 'organum,' the 'formula,' the 'clavis,' the 'ars ipsa interpretandi naturam,' the 'filum Labyrinthi,' or by whichever of its many names we choose to call that artificial process by which alone he believed that man could attain a knowledge of the laws and a command over the powers of nature,—of this philosophy we can make nothing. If we have not tried it, it is because we feel confident that it would not answer. We regard it as a curious piece of machinery, very subtle, elaborate, and ingenious, but not worth constructing, because all the work it could do may be done more easily another way. But though this, the favorite child of Bacon's genius which he would fain have made heir of all he had, died thus in the cradle, his genius itself still lives and works among us; whatever brings us into nearer communion with that is still interesting, and it is as a product and exponent of Bacon's own mind and character that the Baconian philosophy, properly so called, retains its chief value for modern men."

And thus, its Head-light, the "Formula," in abeyance; and with vital parts misplaced, is the work of the greatest genius of the ages swept to the ash pit, as by a wave of the hand.

As in the work of critics, the first makes the road, so the rest meekly tread therein. Having admitted his inability to open the system, Mr. Spedding then pronounces it worthless, saying its work may be done more easily another way. From this kind of criticism we feel it our duty to dissent. This is Shaksperian.

We have here an admirable illustration of Bacon's own words who says: "It is the custom of the human mind, when it either does not comprehend a subject, or has not the ability to comprehend it, to at once place itself above, or to ignore it."

Do any of Bacon's critics know, or pretend to know, the contents of his "Formula of Interpretation" which he so carefully reserved to a private succession? Hence this new system of induction has been so criticised, without having it, as not only to belittle its author, but to stay all further interest in or concerning it. His critics have had but the Lamp, the "New Organ," into which as a light, it was to enter.

Had Bacon, in his own day, made public this Key, the "Formula," or the knowledge how to find "the simple natures" it would have revealed untimely the "Alphabet" and so his secret scheme for posterity, as well as to have endangered his own life. He himself says: "But I account the use that a man should seek of the publication of his own writings before his death, to be an untimely anticipation of that which is proper to follow a man, and not to go along with him."

The earmarks of secrecy are spread throughout Bacon's philosophic writings; and brood over every egg in the nest of Sonnets here under review.

Having by reason of the misplaced parts, like others floundered in the open sea, as to method; we delight thus to relieve the future student, and soon to indicate the true place of entrance to the Baconian system, which hitherto has not been done.

Fearing the "New Organ" might be lost by his untimely death, as Bacon himself tells us, he caused it to be published while yet incomplete. The undated, misplaced parts were surely written subsequent to it; and were but further aid in the opening of it, and of his designs concerning it. Thus far these undated parts have been treated as abandoned fragments, and as if written prior to 1605. They were written in Latin. This was not done with Bacon's early work, and if abandoned, why so print them?

They show that the already mentioned Key, or "Formula of Interpretation" which was to minister to the reason was not to be made public, but was to be reserved to a private succession. They show detailed instructions to the Interpreter. They distinctly show that Bacon was not yet ready to reveal his method of finding the "simple natures."

Save the mentioned juvenile work, "The Noblest Birth of Time," and the "Advancement of Learning" published in 1605; little we judge was written by Bacon on philosophy, save the "New Organ," prior to his fall in 1621. The different parts of his "Natural History," including his "Silva Silvarum," were all written, as was his "New Atlantis," subsequent to that event. The different parts of his "Natural History," when brought into relation, were to be he tells us "The Mother History." This History he called "the bosom to philosophy." The "New Organ," the babe, in Hamlet, was to draw "natures sweet milk, philosophy" from that bosom—from that History, reader. This philosophy, though we are the first to lay the claim, takes its origin in Bacon's investigation of light, which he calls "God's first creature." So in his subtle doctrine of forms, light is God's first form or law. His example of "freeing a direction" to find that law or form we have already touched at p. 68.

Concerning the subject of light, Bacon held distinctive views. He says: "To descend from spiritual and intellectual, to sensible and material forms; we read the first created form was light." He says: "For neither in perspective nor otherwise has any inquiry been made about Light which is of any value. The radiations of it are handled, not the origins. But it is the placing of perspective among the mathematics that has caused this defect, and others of the kind; for thus a premature departure has been made from Physics. Again the manner in which Light and its causes are handled in Physics is somewhat superstitious, as if it were a thing half way between things divine and things natural; insomuch that some of the Platonists have made it older than matter itself; asserting upon a most vain notion that when space was spread forth it was filled first with light, and afterwards with body; whereas the Holy Scriptures distinctly state that there was a dark mass of heaven and earth before light was created." "Phil. Works," Vol. 4, p. 403. These distinctive views as to light, and its origin, will be found in identity when we reach Milton in Chapter 4.

It may thus be seen that Bacon considered light as he did other parts of operating nature.

He begins his investigation in transparent bodies. He moves at once to whiteness, which is the union of all colors, by an orderly change in the configuration of their particles as by pounding glass, or whipping water to a foam.

This orderly inequality, or configuration, is taught in his 27 Prerogative Instances. What relation if any exists between them and the "Alphabet?" As a Prerogative Instance, as of heat, is the controlling instance, is it not also the form? And so of the rest. This emphasis concerning the "Alphabet" will be found important later on in Chapter 5.

The 1st Prerogative Instance called the "Solitary Instance," begins with light, or a transparent body, and the system opens here in uncolored substance. What wonder lies in colors. If you remove all color from a body, what do you to the body? "All color is but the broken image of light," says Bacon. We will touch Bacon on "Substance" when we reach Milton.

Having now in Sonnet 59 and others touched to relation the "New Organ;" and in Sonnet 122 its tables; we here in Sonnets 52 and 65 touch "Time's Best Jewel" its "Formula," or Key. In Sonnet 52 the author says:

SO am I as the rich, whose blessed key
Can bring him to his sweet up-locked treasure,
The which he will not every hour survey,
For blunting the fine point of seldom pleasure.
Therefore are feasts so solemn and so rare,
Since, seldom coming, in the long year set,

> Like stones of worth they thinly placed are,
> Or captain jewels in the carcanet.
> So is the time that keeps you as my chest,
> Or as the wardrobe which the robe doth hide,
> To make some special instant special blest,
> By new unfolding his imprison'd pride.
>> Blessed are you, whose worthiness gives scope,
>> Being had, to triumph, being lack'd, to hope."

Touching this "robe," mantle, or garment of the mind, and the retailoring of it, we shall later have something to say in Chapter 5. In the "Pilgrim's Progress" poem we touch this garment thus:

> "The prophets used much by metaphors
> To set forth truth: yea, who so considers
> Christ, his apostles too, shall plainly see
> That truths to this day in such mantles be."

In the "Holy War" poem:

> "Nor do thou go to work without my Key,
> In mysteries men soon do lose their way."

As to "garment" Bacon says: "Behavior is as a garment and it has all of the conditions of a garment." Again, "For behavior is but a garment, and it is easy to make a comely garment for a body that is itself well-proportioned, whereas a deformed body can never be so helped by tailor's art but the counterfeit will appear." The "tailor's art" will be touched later.

When Sonnet 65, next quoted, was written, Bacon doubtless remained as yet uncertain how to bear this "Formula," this new light—"Time's best jewel"—securely to posterity. It is in these words:

HIS COMPOSED WONDER

SINCE brass, nor stone, nor earth, nor boundless sea,
But sad mortality o'ersways their power,
How with this rage shall beauty hold a plea,
Whose action is no stronger than a flower?
O, how shall summer's honey breath hold out
Against the wreckful siege of battering days,
When rocks impregnable are not so stout,
Nor gates of steel so strong, but Time decays?
O fearful meditation! where, alack,
Shall Time's best jewel from Time's chest lie hid?
Or what strong hand can hold his swift foot back?
Or who his spoil of beauty can forbid?
   O, none, unless this miracle have might,
   That in black ink my love may still shine bright."

"The verses of a poet endure without a syllable lost," says Bacon.

The mentioned Key—"Time's best jewel"—the "Formula," was later, we think, securely placed and will yet be recovered. Note "Time's chest" in Sonnets 48, 52, and 65. The Key was not yet in it. See Sonnet 65.

The author's jewels were his literary works. They in Sonnet 48 are said to have been trifles to the King, yet to the author his greatest comfort. After his fall—"mine only care." His love for them kept him living. See Sonnet 66.

This "care" gave efforts to protect himself, and them from "confounding age's cruel knife" as indicated in Sonnets 19, 63, and 64. In Sonnet 63 he says:

AGAINST my love shall be, as I am now,
With Time's injurious hand crush'd and o'erworn;
When hours have drain'd his blood and fill'd his brow
With lines and wrinkles; when his youthful morn

Hath travell'd on to age's steepy night,
And all those beauties whereof now he's king
Are vanishing or vanish'd out of sight,
Stealing away the treasure of his spring;
For such a time do I now fortify
Against confounding age's cruel knife,
That he shall never cut from memory
My sweet love's beauty, though my lover's life:
  His beauty shall in these black lines be seen,
  And they shall live, and he in them still green."

That the author's beauty inheres in his doings, his works, appears in the Sonnet under review, where we have:

  "His beauty shall in these black lines be seen,
  And they shall live, and he in them still green."

Both the lover's "beauty" and the lover's "life" are here touched. We have his "robe" of beauty in Sonnet 52, which the Key is to open. In this "robe" would he be "beauty's pattern to succeeding men"—Sonnet 19. The Key was the summit of his art.

In the mentioned paper reserving this "Formula" from publication, Bacon says: "And from the injuries of time I am almost secure; but from the injuries of men I am not concerned." He in Sonnet 77 reminds himself of the flight of time, and urges himself anew to his tabular work; and new children of the brain. Note this "continual haste" in Sonnet 123. But how was Francis Bacon almost secure from "the injuries of time?" We answer—"Time's chest." But the Key, the "Formula" was not in it, at the writing of Sonnet 65. Was it ever in the "chest?" When found will it tell where the "chest" is? To tell where the Key, the "Formula" may be found, will be our chief business in Chapter 5.

In the foregoing, we trust we have performed what will some day be found a true and healthful service to the Baconian philosophy, as well as to have rendered to the reader just grounds for the belief that its "Formula of Interpretation" was "Time's best jewel" of Sonnet 65; and that this jewel remains yet in abeyance, and that the system as such must so remain until its recovery, or until some like genius, by aid of existing parts, is able to penetrate the veil.

When the head of this Posthumous has been secured and placed, then, and not till then, may critics rightfully pronounce detractions concerning it.

CHAPTER IV.

FRANCIS BACON'S SHAKE-SPEARE; THE "NOTED WEED" OF SONNET 76. HIS SONNET SENTINELS. NEW LIGHT UPON HIS OVERTHROW. HIS POSTHUMOUS POCKET LABORS. CARLYLE WAIFS FROM THE BACON BUDGET. ELIZABETH'S RIGHTFUL HEIR. IN CONCEALMENT AFTER 1626. WAS COVERT SECRETARY TO CROMWELL AND THE INDEPENDENTS IN THEIR GREAT STRUGGLE. HIS "HOLY WAR," "PILGRIM'S PROGRESS," "MILTON."

IN the foregoing Chapters, we have endeavored to hold back the Shake-speare cover, in order that the reader may view Francis Bacon, the real author, in that scholastic dress, his Shakespeare Sonnets; where, in his own chosen words, he relates, in part, his covert story to posterity. Why he chose to bring forth portions of his work under a cover, or as a Dark Author, involves motives we need not consider here. We leave the reader himself to determine what he meant by his words when he said, "I have (though in a despised weed) procured the good of all men."

Lauding his assumed, his hyphened name, himself behind the mask, Bacon says:

"I, therefore,— will begin;—Soul of the age,
The applause, delight, the wonder of our stage,
My Shakespeare, rise!"

Where says he this? In his Ben Jonson poem introductory to his Plays, where, to his mask, he likewise says:

"Triumph, my Britain! thou hast one to show,
To whom all scenes of Europe homage owe.
He was not of an age, but for all time!"

HIS POSTHUMOUS POCKET LABORS

Reader, carefully note here the subtle and significant words to his Shake-speare, "Thou hast one to show," not yourself, no, but the "He" behind you, the "He" to whom all homage is due, the real author, "our ever living poet" mentioned in the Enigma on the title page of the Sonnets—Bacon himself.

Lauding but his mask, Bacon here preserved his manners in not openly praising himself. How "with manners" he may do this, he indicates in Sonnet 39 by cover word pronouns, where we have:

"O, how thy worth with manners may I sing,
When thou art all the better part of me?
What can mine own praise to mine own self bring?
And what is't but mine own when I praise thee?"

Following his fall, Bacon criticises himself sharply in Sonnet 62 for this self-laudation, this "self-love." He says:

SIN of self-love possesseth all mine eye
And all my soul and all my every part;
And for this sin there is no remedy,
It is grounded inward in my heart.
Methinks no face so gracious is as mine,
No shape so true, no truth of such account;
And for myself mine own worth do define,
As I all other in all worths surmount.
But when my glass shows me myself indeed,
Beated and chopp'd with tann'd antiquity,
Mine own self-love quite contrary I read;
Self so self-loving were iniquity.
  'Tis thee, myself, that for myself I praise,
  Pointing my age with beauty of thy days."

Are not the words of this Sonnet, "no truth of such account," in full accord with the author's great philosophic system? See Sonnet 59, 122, 124 and 125. Whoever he may have been he surely employed a secret method in referring to himself. This will appear in our 7th Division of the Sonnets. By use of the word "myself" in the foregoing Sonnet the author discloses his method. "Tis thee, myself, that for myself I praise."

We come now to the Two Sentinels which for nearly three centuries have guarded this Golden Fleece. They double lock the door. We refer to the 1609 title-page of the Sonnets; and to the, as yet, unsolved Enigma subscribed T. T. appearing later thereon. This Enigma was not found upon the original entry at the stationers; hence the inference. It is now their only title-page; the 1609 date being dropped altogether.

Careful study of their relations, if their words mean anything, makes it certain, see Sonnet 111, 118, 119, 125, 88, 89, 90 and others, that the 1609 entry at the Stationers was either an unauthorized entry; or a most adroit device for future use. As we now have them, they were not in print prior to Bacon's fall in 1621. An edition using the old title-page, or entry, may, it is true, have been made to take the place of the original entry. An unauthorized use of title-pages at about this period, as well upon some of the plays, as upon other writings, was common. "Discovery sooner emerges from error than from confusion"—says Bacon. His ever present motives for concealment will appear later.

The mentioned Enigma has defied thus far any sanctioned interpretation, though much energetic ink has been bestowed upon it. The labored question seems to have been, who was its "Mr. W. H?" It is in these words:

> "TO THE ONLIE BEGETTER OF
> THESE INSUING SONNETS
> MR. W. H. ALL HAPPINESSE
> AND THAT ETERNITIE
> PROMISED BY
> OUR EVER-LIVING POET
> WISHETH
> THE WELL-WISHING
> ADVENTURER IN
> SETTING
> FORTH
> T. T."

For reasons appearing later in Sonnet 81, we say to the reader the eternity here promised, was to Mr. W. Himself, using the letter W for the christian name of the mask, instead of the last, with "H" or the cover word pronoun Himself, and thus used, the better to tangle the sense, or deepen the Enigma.

W is the only letter of the alphabet formed from two letters, U and U, two equals. It is both a co-equal, and a concordant one. In union they are the U U, the two in one, the single one. They are "He" Himself to whom all homage is due in the Ben Jonson poem. When in Sonnet 39 the author inquires how "with manners" he may praise himself and his mission, we here see how, in fact, his subtlety performed it.

Instead of saying Mr. W. S. (William Shakespeare) we have "Mr. W." (that is U. U.) "Himself," the pronoun cover word "Himself" standing in the couplet for both author and mask, in conformity with our 7th Division of the Sonnets. Bacon and his nom de plume, his mask, let it be remembered, stood in a couplet. They were the "co-supremes," and the "concordant one," wherein—

>"So they lov'd, as love in twain
>Had the essence but in one;
>Two distincts, division none:
>Number there in love was slain."

Taken from "The Phoenix and Turtle" the poem with which the Shakespeare writings are brought to conclusion. See Hudson's Shakespeare Vol. 11 p. 238.

The 154 covert tell-tales, or tom-tits, set forth under the Enigma, are, however, the royal nest eggs of their true author, over which time still sits on brood.

That the promise, in the Enigma, of "Our ever living poet" Bacon, to his mask, his Shakespeare, was fulfilled to the letter, see Sonnet 81; where Bacon yields to him not only the honored epitaph and monument, due to himself; but pronounces both in faithful laudation, thus:

OR I shall live your epitaph to make,
　Or you survive when I in earth am rotten;
From hence your memory death cannot take,
Although in me each part will be forgotten.
Your name from hence immortal life shall have,
Though I, once gone, to all the world must die:
The earth can yield me but a common grave,
When you entombed in men's eyes shall lie.
Your monument shall be my gentle verse,
Which eyes not yet created shall o'er-read,
And tongues to be your being shall rehearse
When all the breathers of this world are dead;
　You still shall live—such virtue hath my pen—
　Where breath most breathes, even in the mouths of
　　men."

Reader, is the Enigma interpreted? Was not "that eternity promised" in it, to "Mr. W. H." fulfilled to the letter, in this Sonnet 81? It tells the reader, if language means anything, that there are two persons concerned in it; that one of the persons is to have but a common grave; and that it is the pen of the one who is to have but the common grave, that makes the monument for the other; and this whether or not he lives to make his epitaph.

To make sure now to the reader that a couplet, or two persons are concerned in it, we further quote Sonnet 36:

LET me confess that we two must be twain,
Although our undivided loves are one:
So shall those blots that do with me remain
Without thy help by me be borne alone.
In our two loves there is but one respect,
Though in our lives a separable spite,
Which though it alter not love's sole effect,
Yet doth it steal sweet hours from love's delight.
I may not evermore acknowledge thee,
Lest my bewailed guilt should do thee shame,
Nor thou with public kindness honour me,
Unless thou take that honour from thy name:
    But do not so; I love thee in such sort
    As, thou being mine, mine is thy good report."

Sonnet 39 should be here read, touching this couplet, as should the already mentioned "Phoenix and Turtle." By aid of his mask Bacon held aloft his name to a future day, well knowing if he assumed immediate authorship, following his fall, it must of necessity bring ruin, not only upon the prepared, but upon his yet to be prepared, labors for posterity. In Sonnet 55 he promises himself immortality in fame, when a true judgment of himself has been made. Let its pronouns be read in the first person.

In our "Defoe Period" p. 114 we were first to lay the claim that all the poems introductory to the plays, though other names are appended to them, were still products of Bacon's own pen. This is likewise true of the Shakespeare epitaph. It is in these strange words:

"Good friend, for Jesus' sake forbear
To dig the dust inclosed here:
Blest be the man that spares these stones,
And curst be he that moves my bones."

Was there no ulterior purpose here, reader, lurking behind this strange prohibition? Though it may have been abandoned for some later method, still, the words of the epitaph seem to us as designed to fix a point or monument from which measurements might, at some future day, be taken. And where, please, was "Time's chest" of Sonnet 65 to find its ultimate resting place? See, please, Chapter 3, p. 75 to 78.

The greater part of Bacon's literary career from early years was evidently spent on the dark side of the line. This prepared him for that noted readiness and brevity displayed in all his attributed work. In a literary way he evidently purposed to out-do all that had gone before him, Homer not excepted.

His minute observation, his fabulous memory, together with the rapidity and subtlety of his comprehension, made him a literary wonder; and in a sense not yet revealed; and he remained long at labor.

Book 6 of his "De Augmentis" in four Chapters should here be read in full, and studied; if the reader would fully realize Bacon's great posterity secret. See "Phil. Works" by Spedding Vol. 4, p. 438 to 498. It concerns the use of cyphers, and the handing on of writings to posterity. As to his own great Bi-literal Cypher p. 445, he says: "But for avoiding suspicion altogether, I will add another contrivance, which I devised myself when I was at Paris in my early youth, and which I still think worthy of preservation. For it has the perfection of a cypher, which is to make anything signify anything; subject, however, to this condition, that the infolding writing shall contain at least five times as many letters as the writing infolded; no other condition or restriction whatever is required." In the paragraph opening its first Chapter he says: "And certainly I have raised up here a little heap of dust, and stored under it a great many grains of sciences and arts; into which the ants may creep and rest for a while, and then prepare themselves for fresh labors. Now the wisest of Kings refers sluggards to the ants; and for my part I hold all men for sluggards who care only to use what they have got, without preparing for new seed times and new harvests of knowledge." From this Chapter Mrs. Gallup's great work entitled "Francis Bacon's Bi-literal Cypher" to which we shall later have occasion to refer, takes its origin.

Before entering upon the facts themselves involved in Bacon's overthrow, we permit him some further words in addition to those set forth in Chapter 2.

Throughout his entire career he was notably silent as to any injuries done to himself. This fact should be considered in estimating his character. Happenings to himself he ever attributes, either to providence, or fortune. See, please, in our "Defoe Period," p. 76 to 90, what he says of providence and fortune. Fortune, in the plays he calls a strumpet. And, in Sonnet 111, we have:

O for my sake do you with Fortune chide,
The guilty goddess of my harmful deeds,
That did not better for my life provide
Than public means which public manners breeds.
Thence comes it that my name receives a brand,
And almost thence my nature is subdued
To what it works in, like the dyer's hand:
Pity me then and wish I were renew'd;
Whilst, like a willing patient, I will drink
Potions of eisel 'gainst my strong infection;
No bitterness that I will bitter think,
Nor double penance, to correct correction.
  Pity me then, dear friend, and I assure ye
  Even that your pity is enough to cure me."

The author in this Sonnet laments his entry into public life. What relation can it bear, reader, to the life doings of the man Shaksper? In this Sonnet, in Sonnet 62 and 110 the author becomes his own self critic.

As to this guilty goddess "Fortune," see now, please, Sonnets 25, 29, 37 and 90.

In Sonnet 68 the author says the times are bad, and that their "signs of fair" are but "bastards." See also Sonnet 127 wherein he refers to time, or the times, as his mistress. And in Sonnet 67 he, as to both the times, and himself, says:

AH! wherefore with infection should he live,
And with his presence grace impiety,
That sin by him advantage should achieve
And lace itself with his society?
Why should false painting imitate his cheek

And steal dead seeing of his living hue?
Why should poor beauty indirectly seek
Roses of shadow, since his rose is true?
Why should he live, now Nature bankrupt is,
Beggar'd of blood to blush through lively veins?
For she hath no exchequer now but his,
And, proud of many, lives upon his gains.
  O, him she stores, to show what wealth she had
  In days long since, before these last so bad."

We now permit the author, whoever he may have been, to tell his own story concerning his guilt. As we have seen, Bacon said, "I am not guilty to myself of any unworthiness, except perhaps too much softness at the beginning of my troubles." And the author of Sonnet 121 says:

'TIS better to be vile than vile esteem'd,
  When not to be receives reproach of being,
And the just pleasure lost which is so deem'd
Not by our feeling but by others' seeing:
For why should others' false adulterate eyes
Give salutation to my sportive blood?
Or on my frailties why are frailer spies,
Which in their wills count bad what I think good?
No, I am that I am, and they that level
At my abuses reckon up their own:
I may be straight, though they themselves be bevel;
By their rank thoughts my deeds must not be shown;
  Unless this general evil they maintain,
  All men are bad, and in their badness reign."

The reader should not fail to read attentively what the author says to the King in Sonnets 35, 49, 58, 88, 89, 118 and 125, touching the question of his guilt here under review. In the last quoted Sonnet, "By their rank thoughts my deeds must not be shown" will appear the Author's entire disbelief in obtaining justice by any attempted defense. His efforts to secure pardon had failed. The King's dalliance and delay in it, find expression in Sonnets 57 and 58. In Sonnet 58 he says:

WHAT God forbid that made me first your slave,
I should in thought control your times of pleasure,
Or at your hand the account of hours to crave,
Being your vassal, bound to stay your leisure !
O, let me suffer, being at your beck,
The imprison'd absence of your liberty;
And patience, tame to sufferance, bide each check,
Without accusing you of injury.
Be where you list, your charter is so strong
That you yourself may privilege your time
To what you will; to you it doth belong
Yourself to pardon of self-doing crime.
 I am to wait, though waiting so be hell;
 Nor blame your pleasure, be it ill or well."

The author of this Sonnet says to the King it was God "that made me first your slave," having opened the previous Sonnet in the words,

"Being your slave what should I do but tend
 Upon the hours and times of your desire?"

The opening word "What" of the foregoing Sonnet is in some editions printed "That." The offense that needs pardon, is in this Sonnet said to be the King's own.

If asked on what authority these Sonnets and these words apply to a King, we answer, the Author's own words in Sonnet 57, wherein we have "Whilst I, my sovereign, watch the clock for you."

The King's hypnotism over the author was at its height at the writing of Sonnets 112, 113 and others. His ultimate, though not open breach with him, began in Sonnet 87. And he closes Sonnet 147 touching the King thus:

"For I have sworn thee fair and thought thee bright,
Who art as black as hell, as dark as night."

If the reader would know something of the true inwardness of this King James I., as developed near the close of his reign, let him read attentively Chapter 16, Vol. 3 of "Knight's History of England."

We come now to the covert causes which were involved in Francis Bacon's overthrow. They have not been touched by others, so far as we know. Attention at the outset is invited to Sonnet 120; and to its covert words to the King "To weigh how once I suffer'd in your crime." It is in these words:

"THAT you were once unkind befriends me now,
And for that sorrow which I then did feel
Needs must I under my transgression bow,
Unless my nerves were brass or hammer'd steel.
For if you were by my unkindness shaken
As I by yours, you've pass'd a hell of time,
And I, a tyrant, have no leisure taken
To weigh how once I suffer'd in your crime.
O, that our night of woe might have remember'd
My deepest sense, how hard true sorrow hits,
And soon to you, as you to me, then tender'd
The humble salve which wounded bosoms fits!
  But that your trespass now becomes a fee;
  Mine ransoms yours, and yours must ransom me."

Earlier we have noted the King's feigned tears at the opening of Bacon's troubles, p. 37. During this period Bacon in a letter to Mathews says: "I would not have my friends (though I know it to be out of love) too apprehensive either of me, or for me; for I thank God my ways are sound and good, and I hope God will bless me in them. When once my master, and afterwards myself, were both of us in extremity of sickness (which was no time to dissemble) I never had so great pledges and certainties of his love and favour: and that which I knew then, such as took a little poor advantage of these latter times, know since." "Bacon's Letters" by Spedding, Vol. 7, p. 201.

Let the reader contrast this letter and its guarded closing words, with the Sonnet under review, especially with its words "To weigh how once I suffer'd in your crime."

Read then Bacon's letter written at the close of the Somerset trial, just before the King left for Scotland. "Bacon's Letters," Vol. 5, p. 347. We claim to the reader that the words of this Sonnet "To weigh how once I suffer'd in your crime," are Bacon's own words to the King touching the death of Sir Thomas Overbury in the Tower in 1616.

When Somerset, the then King's favorite, was arrested for the crime, he was found in company with the King who was lolling his arms about his neck, and kissing him. Departing, the King said, "Now the Deel go with thee for I will never see thy face any more." "Knight's History of England," Vol. 3, p. 300. Devices were used by the King to induce Somerset to confess, he declaring the King durst not bring him to trial. "Bacon's Letters," Vol. 5, p. 305, 340 to 346.

HIS POSTHUMOUS POCKET LABORS 93

Was the shielding of the King, upon the trial of this cause, that which "God forbid" in Sonnet 58? Francis Bacon's overthrow took its chief, its tap-root, here, we say, in this noted trial; by reason of an awakened hate, which, though covert, as we shall see, was both bitter, and bottomless. At its beginning Bacon said to the King: "Your Majesty hath put me upon a work of providence in this great cause." He entertained a fixed belief that the Somerset case, at bottom, involved a plot, a new attempt to return England to the old or Catholic faith, by throwing her into the arms of Spain, in connection with the, then on foot Spanish marriage alliance. "Bacon's Letters," Vol. 6, p. 144 to 147. See in this the work of "Northampton and the Undertakers." "Bacon's Letters," Vol. 5, p. 41 to 48, and p. 71 to 74; and Vol. 6, p. 144 to 187; Vol. 4, p. 283. See, then, please, Vol. 7, p. 369.

This had been earlier sought during the reign of Elizabeth, by the Queen of Scots, the King's mother, a staunch supporter of the Catholic faith; but averted by her execution largely through plottings and by fear of the event.

At the close of the Somerset trial, the King ran at once to Scotland, making first, a sweeping proclamation, ordering all the nobility and gentry from London into the country and done evidently to quell the strange gossip which the case had aroused at what was then called "A Popish plot."

Coke, Bacon, and the nobility, had learned too much already in this strange trial, touching the King himself. Rumor said his hand was deep in the business. See "Knight's History of England," Vol. 3, p. 243 to 367. "Bacon's Letters," Vol. 5, p. 337, 341 and 344.

Coke and Bacon must now be awed—placed beneath the hatchet—and rumor quelled. This was the diplomacy of James. This he did to the finish, by first pitting Bacon against Coke, whose mouth had been too open during the trial; and then, later, by Coke against Bacon. Being at known enmity with each other, this was the more easily effected, by the King, without disclosing his motives. And what did make the author of Sonnet 58, whoever he was, the King's slave? What was the "self-doing crime" of that Sonnet? And why had the King "tongue-tied" the author of Sonnet 140?

Francis Bacon's overthrow must ere long be placed in the open, having slept now nearly three centuries. The secret three headed combine called in Sonnet 137 "a several plot" will yet take air.

Though not without faults, who is? still, the bribery charges against Bacon we regard but as a color; a pretext. They would neither have been made, nor have prevailed, had it not been for that which lay behind, reader. Bribery charges were not presented until after Bacon was fully within the trap, let it be remembered; he having been first charged as one of certain Referees in other matters which the King purposed not to have opened. See, please, "Bacon's Letters," Vol. 7, p. 195 to 199 and 184 to 209. After some skirmishing the business of the Referees was totally abandoned, bribery charges against him taking its place. That Bacon had been promised full pardon, to forego his defense, see his own words, Chapter 2, p. 41. He had no trial, but was compelled now to a particularized statement. He gave not this until he saw the King's hand joined with his enemies. He was then made to realize what the plotters unalterably proposed to have, and he gave it, as the shortest and safeest way. The business of the Referees concerned, we say, "the South Sea," a secret thwarted Baconian project for revenue, tacked to his "New Atlantis," which had long been carried in smother, and wherein many Englishmen had lost their money. It was thwarted by his enemies, and sharpers. It will be touched later. Instead of the "New Atlantis," not published until 1627, being a Baconian vision, we say it was a secret organization of his own day, with a membership of the best blood of England, but so secret as to be almost unknown, save by his own words. In its closing paragraph he says, "We are here in God's bosom a land unknown." Later we think it engaged in Buckingham's impeachment, and in Bacon's great posterity project. Touching "the South Sea" and the mentioned scheme, we from "As You Like It," Act 3, Sc. 2, quote thus: "Ros. Good my complexion! dost thou think, though I am caparison'd like a man, I have a doublet and hose in my disposition? One inch of delay more is a South-sea of discovery. I pr'ythee, tell me, who is it? quickly, and speak apace. I would thou couldst stammer, that thou might'st pour this conceal'd man out of thy mouth, as wine comes out of a narrow-mouth'd bottle; either too much at once, or none at all. I pr'ythee, take the cork out of thy mouth, that I may drink thy tidings."

It has been thought that Bacon was unaware of his danger until charges were actually preferred against him. On the contrary, just before the Parliament convened wherein he met his overthrow, he opens a letter to the King thus: "May it please your Majesty, I thank God that I number my days both in thankfulness to Him and in warning to myself." See "Bacon's Letters," Vol. 7, p. 168.

The purpose of this letter doubtless was to strengthen the King in his favor, and to intimate, what he then anticipated. He was aware of the undercurrent, of envy, that was mining for him, though not, we think, of its scope.

Let us now look at some of the motives that lay back of this movement; and first at the tap-root motive. Following the mentioned Somerset trial, and while the King was still absent in Scotland, Bacon was warned by letter from a friend who came fresh from an interview with both King and Buckingham. This warning letter should be read in full. From it we quote points three and four, thus:

"3rd. That it is too common in every man's mouth in court, that your greatness shall be abated, and as your tongue hath been as a razor to some, so shall theirs be to you.

"4th. That there is laid up for you, to make your burden the more grievous, many petitions to his Majesty against you."

The letter closes with "I beseech your Lordship burn this letter." "Bacon's Letters," Vol. 6, p. 248.

But in what, please, had Francis Bacon's tongue been "a razor to some?" Much might be said here. Space permits us little more than to touch it. We here but outline.

In his charge, in the Somerset trial, Bacon, among other things said: "For impoisonment, I am sorry it should be heard of in this kingdom: it is not *nostri generis nec sanguinis*: it is an Italian crime, fit for the court of Rome, where that person that intoxicateth the Kings of the earth with his cup of poison in heretical doctrine, is many times really and materially intoxicated and impoisoned himself." "Bacon's Letters," Vol. 5, p. 309, and see page 44, 72, 162, and 165.

Note what he said on this trial touching Northampton. He had been the most powerful person in the government of James, and was in full accord with the Romish church.

Again, in a charge to the Judges while the King was still in Scotland, Bacon said, "Now to some particulars, and not many. Of all other things I must begin as the King begins; that is, with the cause of religion; and especially the hollow church-papist. St. Augustin hath a good comparison of such men, affirming that they are like the roots of nettles, which themselves sting not, but yet they bear all the stinging leaves. Let me know of such roots, and I will root them out of the country." "Bacon's Letters," Vol. 6, p. 213. Throughout the plays note the use of this word "nettle" and "nettle danger."

Buckingham, whose mother was a Catholic, succeeded Somerset as King's favorite. Upon becoming such, Bacon in a letter of advice to him, says: "Take heed, I beseech you, that you be no instrument to countenance the Romish Catholics, nor the religion professed by them. I cannot flatter you; the world, Sir, believes that some near in blood to you are too much of that persuasion; you may use them with fit respects, according to the bond of nature; you are of kin, and so must be a friend to their persons, but not to their errors." "Bacon's Letters," Vol. 6, p. 31.

The long Expostulatory Letter to Coke should be read here in full. Though not subscribed, it was surely Bacon's as Coke, Buckingham, the King, and others were well aware. Spedding does not think it his, and gives it but in part. "Bacon's Letters," Vol. 6, p. 121.

The burden of this anonymous letter, was a Popish Plot behind the Somerset business. It is a biting criticism upon Coke, for his indiscreet acts on the trial. It claims that they averted the opening of the Plot. Coke, from the bench, p. 125, at the beginning of the trial among other strange things said: "I think next the gunpowder treason there was never such a plot as this is. I could discover knights, great men and others."

As already stated Bacon believed the business involved a new attempt to return England to the old faith, in connection with the then on foot Spanish marriage, backed by Northampton and others, and that Overbury became possessed of the secret, and so was run quickly to the Tower.

It may clearly be seen from the foregoing in what Bacon's tongue had become "a razor to some." For a considerable period of time, he had, with great subtlety, stood athwart the ripening of events. "The church is the eye of England;" says Bacon. He says: "Divinity is the art of arts."

Every investigation into the life and doings of Francis Bacon will be found defective that fails to recognize the fact that he had ever his forefinger upon the world's pulse ecclesiastic; and that until after his fall, he was a believer in the doctrine of passive obedience, and the divine right of Kings.

Later the opportunity came, and Rome, or its adherents, made even with Bacon for calling them "nettles," and their belief "the sore of time," as he does both in and out of the plays. See as to "nettle-seed" our "Defoe Period," p. 327. We must present the causes involved in Francis Bacon's overthrow, as they appear to us. The reader must judge.

HIS POSTHUMOUS POCKET LABORS 99

The second cause involved in the "several plot" for his overthrow, was Coke and his adherents, endeavoring to beat back this doctrine of passive obedience. The third cause was his thwarted revenue scheme wherein many Englishmen lost their money. These losses we understand to be the "harmful deeds" of Sonnet 111. Let your globes of vision rest here, Reader. See p. 100. It was tacked, we say, to his "New Atlantis." His carefully prepared speech to Parliament concerning it, should be read here in full. It may be found in our "Defoe Period" page 20 to 23. Mr. Spedding fails to give it. See, please, what he says concerning it. "Bacon's Letters," Vol. 7, p. 199, 200, 235. Note page 189, and 190, that Bacon had been sent for by the King. We will have occasion to quote from it later.

Did Bacon's lost, or kept out of sight, budget of April 25th, 1615, concern it? See "Bacon's Letters," Vol. 5, p. 129 and 130. And was there a fixed and settled purpose to keep them concealed, reader?

As to England, the King was a foreigner, and was lavish in his expenditure of money. Parliament, to the time of Bacon's overthrow, had persistently neglected or refused to supply him with money, unless he would surrender certain prerogatives. To supply his necessities England's Treasury, now and for a long time had been placed in commission. "Bacon's Letters," Vol. 6, p. 317 and Vol. 7, p. 1. Bacon ever urged the King to rely upon Parliament for means. But the Undertakers following the defeat of Salisbury's scheme in 1612, backed by Northampton and others, boggled, and thwarted; and the King in anger dissolved without relief; each and every of his Parliaments to the one wherein Francis Bacon met his overthrow in 1621.

The business of this commission, let it be remembered, consisted in devising and carrying out revenue projects. Salisbury's, known as the "great contract," had been carried to open, and had failed. It had noised abroad, to Spain, and elsewhere, the King's wants. Bacon's scheme for revenue backed by his "New Atlantis," was now to follow a different method. It was to be carried and managed with the utmost secrecy. Let the Defoe "Essay on Projects" be called here to its true place in this literature. See Addison on projects, Vol. 4, page 198 to 202.

When the bottom of this secret scheme is reached, reader, the mystery surrounding Raleigh's voyage, and his subtle taking off and the King's methods in it, will be in the open. Why went it so in smother? Did the King impose silence here? Who put up the 40,000 pound bond for the faithful performance of Raleigh's trust? See "Bacon's Letters," Vol. 6, p. 343, 345 and 349. And whose property ultimately went to satisfy those Englishmen who had so lost their money, in that thwarted "New Atlantis" scheme? Again, whose tongues were tied, following its defeat? See Sonnet 140 and our presentation at p. 41 to 45.

This investigation should be the work of our projected Society. Let Bacon's labors in 1618 be here looked into, wherein he sought now to adjust this his secret revenue scheme into relation with England's treasury. He first signed his name here as Francis Verulam. "Bacon's Letters," Vol. 6, p. 317. Note following it, his letter to the King, p. 452.

This thwarted revenue scheme came not to light, reader, until an attempt to re-enact it in the Defoe Period; and then not as Bacon's. It, and the prepared literature concerning it, belongs with Bacon's Posthumous Pocket labors. These papers concern reform, and were aids

HIS POSTHUMOUS POCKET LABORS 101

in placing the English Constitution upon its true ancient foundation. They consist of the mentioned Defoe "Essay on Projects;" Essay on "The South Sea Trade;" on "The Six Distinguishing Characters of a Parliament Man;" "Considerations Upon Corrupt Elections of Members to Serve in Parliament;" "The Freeholders Plea Against Stock-jobbing;" "Elections of Parliament Men;" "The Succession of the Crown of England Considered;" "The Villany of Stock Jobbers Detected and the Causes of the Late Run upon the Bank and Bankers Discovered and Considered;" "The Dangers to the Protestant Religion Considered from the Present Prospect of a Religious War in Europe;" "The Original Power of the Collective Body of the People of England Examined and Asserted;" and others. These brief pamphlets came from Francis Bacon's own hand we say, during the period now under review. They were part of his posterity labors, and were played out later.

As to "Considerations upon Corrupt Elections of Members to Serve in Parliament," see now "Bacon's Letters," Vol. 5, p. 19 to 24, and 52 to 75, also 161 to 191. We could give many references. See Vol. 7, p. 116, 127, 183. As to "The Six Distinguishing Characters of a Parliament Man," see, please, "Bacon's Letters," Vol. 5, p. 176 to 191.

As to the "Dutch" and the "Catastrophe" itself, of Bacon's thwarted revenue or "South Sea Scheme;" see please our "Defoe Period" page 475 to 478. As to the "Dutch" and this same "Catastrophe" see Bacon's Letter dated November 26th, 1619. "Bacon's Letters," Vol. 7, p. 63. It is again touched on page 76. Note its allusion to "the jolly letter from Zealand, and the King's dislike of it." Note please in these letters, Bacon's covert air of secrecy. See page 181 to 191; and Vol. 7, p. 116, 127, 183.

"The Newly Discovered Defoe Papers" should be introduced here to the reader. Later we will call them to relation with Bacon's great "Alphabet of Nature." Throughout, they present a distinctive uncalled for use of capital letters, and are all works in cypher. See in this our "Defoe Period" page 447 to 520. Touching the question of revenue, see, please, page 462 to 475 and 501 to 507.

Having earlier touched to relation the triple cause involved in Francis Bacon's overthrow, we here introduce the subtle Sonnet 137, which directly concerns it. It is called "a several plot." And the author to himself here says:

THOU blind fool, Love, what dost thou to mine eyes,
That they behold, and see not what they see?
They know what beauty is, see where it lies,
Yet what the best is take the worst to be.
If eyes corrupt by over-partial looks
Be anchor'd in the bay where all men ride,
Why of eyes' falsehood hast thou forged hooks,
Whereto the judgment of my heart is tied?
Why should my heart think that a several plot
Which my heart knows the wide world's common place?
Or mine eyes seeing this, say this is not,
To put fair truth upon so foul a face?
   In things right true my heart and eyes have erred,
   And to this false plague are they now tranferr'd."

Let "mine eye" of Sonnet 113 be called into relation with "mine eyes" of this Sonnet. The author's hypnotism, his love, is in this Sonnet, said to be a "blind fool;"

in Sonnet 57 a true fool; in Sonnet 147 it is as a fever; and in Sonnet 119 it is said to be ruined and new built. In the foregoing Sonnet, the author sharply criticises the folly of his love, in not heeding the "several plot."

Touching now its "false plague," we from Bacon's Letter to Buckingham at the beginning of his troubles, quote thus:

"Your Lordship spake of purgatory. I am now in it, but my mind is in a calm; for my fortune is not my felicity. I know I have clean hands and a clean heart; and I hope a clean house for friends or servants. But Job himself, or whosoever was the justest judge by such hunting for matters against him as hath been used against me, may for a time seem foul, specially in a time when greatness is the mark and accusation is the game. And if this be to be a Chancellor, I think if the great seal lay upon Hounslow Heath, nobody would take it up." "Bacon's Letters," Vol. 7, p. 213. This letter, which has no date, was written we judge after the business of the Referees had been abandoned, for the bribery charges; and when Bacon first found himself fully within the trap. Touching the plot itself of the foregoing Sonnet, see the play of "The Tempest," Act 4, Sc. 1, which first appeared in the folio of 1623.

A man's character is what he in fact is; his reputation simply what people believe him to be; on either true or false testimony. The suave letters and speeches of Francis Bacon to those whom he well knew were seeking his ruin, have, we think, greatly befogged the estimate thus far made of him. To this must be added withheld, tampered with, and many undated, misplaced papers. The question which here confronts us is, may one without guilt, pit subtlety against subtlety to preserve honor, and the sequestration of property, in the face of a known determined purpose for his overthrow? See Sonnet 90, as to this "purposed overthrow."

When Bacon saw the King's hand, joined with his enemies, he realized that defense would be futile; and at once assumed the attitude towards him, in which he placed Cranmer, in his play of Henry the 8th, Act 5, Sc. 1, where we have:

"Cran.   Most dread liege,
  The good I stand on is my truth and honesty;
  If they shall fail, I, with mine enemies,
  Will triumph o'er my person, which I weigh not,
  Being of those virtues vacant, I fear nothing
  What can be said against me."

A little further on he says:

"Cran.   God and your majesty
  Protect mine innocence, or I fall into
  The trap is laid for me."

Having at the instance of the King abandoned his defence as indicated in Sonnets 49 and 125, Bacon was soon made to realize where his pet doctrine of passive obedience placed him, in the hands of such a King. And so in Sonnet 118 he says, it "brought to medicine a healthful state."

Let this King's kissing and lolling of arms about the neck of Somerset upon his arrest be called to relation with "your ne'er cloying sweetness" of this Sonnet. See its words "Drugs poison him that so fell sick of you." p. 40.

When the flush of Bacon's sorrow had passed, he reviewed the situation. From the King's "ne'er cloying sweetness," and from his broken bed-rock vow of pardon, referred to in Sonnet 152, Bacon broke forth to a new dawning, to "a second life on second head" as stated in Sonnet 68, where the good days of Queen Elizabeth are contrasted with the "bastard signs of fair" of those of James the 1st. This Sonnet must ever mark the beginning of Francis Bacon's new or second literary period. It is in these words:

> THUS is his cheek the map of days outworn,
> When beauty lived and died as flowers do now,
> Before these bastard signs of fair were born,
> Or durst inhabit on a living brow;
> Before the olden tresses of the dead,
> The right of sepulchres, were shorn away,
> To live a second life on second head;
> Ere beauty's dead fleece made another gay:
> In him those holy antique hours are seen,
> Without all ornament, itself and true,
> Making no summer of another's green,
> Robbing no old to dress his beauty new;
>   And him as for a map doth Nature store,
>   To show false Art what beauty was of yore."

The "signs of fair" of James' government are here said to be "bastards," at least, you have here Bacon's own words for it, reader, and it is his story we are trying to let him tell.

"The olden tresses of the dead" clearly alludes to Queen Elizabeth, under whose reign men in safety "lived and died as flowers do now." As to "the right of sepulchres." If now Bacon was the son of Leicester and the Queen, by a valid secret marriage, as claimed in his own Bi-literal Cypher, then, as already stated, the first eighteen purposeful Sonnets may be justly regarded as an adroit urging upon the Queen to declare or proclaim his own lawful right to the throne, as her successor; well knowing she would or could not wed. As she could not be induced to do this, so "the right of sepulchres were shorn away." The cypher story says that early in her reign she agreed to do this. See Mrs. Gallup's Work, p. 351.

Had Bacon been preparing the "fleece," now thought "dead," by reason of his overthrow, with an abiding hope of succession? The new life began now, ere the literary "dead fleece had made another gay." The "dead fleece" evidently alludes to the author's Golden Fleece, his literary work.

Touching now his troubles, and the "second life" of the Sonnet, he in Sonnet 110 says: "These blenches gave my heart another youth."

And he closes Sonnet 109 touching his philosophy thus:

"For nothing this wide universe I call,
Save thou, my rose, in it thou art my all."

In Sonnets 100, 101 and 107 Bacon withdraws his love and duty from the King to his heart's garden, his "love's sweet face," philosophy. And in Sonnet 100 he says:

WHERE art thou, Muse, that thou forget'st so long
    To speak of that which gives thee all thy might?
Spend'st thou thy fury on some worthless song,
Darkening thy power to lend base subjects light?
Return, forgetful Muse, and straight redeem
In gentle numbers time so idly spent;
Sing to the ear that doth thy lays esteem
And gives thy pen both skill and argument.
Rise, resty Muse, my love's sweet face survey,

If Time have any wrinkle graven there;
If any, be a satire to decay,
And make Time's spoils despised every where.
  Give my love fame faster than Time wastes life;
  So thou prevent'st his scythe and crooked knife."

Bacon's "pyramid," his literary temple broken at his fall, is now to be new-reared, rebuilt. Hence he opens Sonnet 123 thus:

"No, Time, thou shalt not boast that I do change
Thy pyramids built up with newer might."

And he closes it with:

"This I do vow and this shall ever be;
I will be true, despite thy scythe and thee."

Bacon himself says of this "pyramid:" "I am not raising a capitol or pyramid to the pride of man, but laying a foundation in the human understanding for a holy temple after the model of the world. That model therefore I follow. For whatever deserves to exist deserves also to be known, for knowledge is the image of existence." "Bacon's Phil. Works," Vol. 4, p. 107. He purposed now to rear to himself an ever enduring monument. This he does in Sonnet 107, believing the greatest durance to live in the words of a poet. At his fall he bestowed it upon his mask, Shakespeare, in Sonnet 81 as we have seen, p. 84.

Now in Sonnet 107 this great reflector of light calls himself "the mortal moon," and says he and his "true love"—his philosophy— have endured their eclipse; and

that he will live in it, when "tombs of brass are spent."
He says:

> NOT mine own fears, nor the prophetic soul
>   Of the wide world dreaming on things to come,
> Can yet the lease of my true love control,
> Supposed as forfeit to a confined doom.
> The mortal moon hath her eclipse endured
> And the sad augurs mock their own presage;
> Incertainties now crown themselves assured
> And peace proclaims olives of endless age.
> Now with the drops of this most balmy time
> My love looks fresh, and Death to me subscribes,
> Since, spite of him, I'll live in this poor rhyme,
> While he insults o'er dull and speechless tribes:
>   And thou in this shall find thy monument,
>   When tyrants' crests and tombs of brass are spent."

For duration, Francis Bacon regarded poetry as the best possible material for constructing a monument, and for proof thereof refers to the writings of Homer, and says: "The monuments of wit survive the monuments of power; the verses of a poet endure without a syllable lost, while States and Empires pass many periods."

The author of the foregoing Sonnet refers to efforts made to thwart his vast reform, his life work—his "true love"—by the ruin of his name. As his ruin was not complete, the "augurs" were sad. They may now "mock" at their predictions concerning it. The hour has past. "Incertainties now crown themselves assured." Touching the "all-oblivious enmity" of the "augurs," see Sonnet 55. His fears concerning it are again touched in Sonnet 119.

That the King, following the Somerset trial, formed a fixed intention to blacken Bacon; to "put some public exemplary mark" of disgrace upon him. See please, "Bacon's Letters," Vol. 6, p. 251 and p. 247 and 8. That the King came to hate him, see the already mentioned Sonnets 89 and 90.

Did he in subtlety later raise him to the desired honors of Verulam and St. Alban that his fall might seem the greater; and the eclipse of his influence the more dense and durable? While professing a different faith, still the King was, at heart, a Catholic as is well known. His mother was the Queen of Scots, and was executed by reason of Papal plottings for the English throne. Touching Buckingham's mother in the business, see the above reference, p. 243 and 321; and our "Defoe Period," p. 344 to 346.

In the Sonnet under review, the author indicates that he—his thoughts—shall at least live in its masked lines and thence his monument, even though death "insults o'er dull and speechless tribes"—that is—tribes through dullness in not discovering the true facts; and hence "speechless" as to the honor due his name. The "dull and speechless tribes" have now endured nearly three centuries, reader.

In his writings Bacon oft alludes to the King, as the sun; and to the moon, as counsel. Touching "eclipse" in this Sonnet we quote him thus: "The fountain of honor is the King, and his aspect and the access to his person continueth honor in life, and to be banished from his presence is one of the greatest eclipses of honor that can be." "Bacon's Letters," Vol. 4, p. 403. See eclipse, please, in Sonnets 33, 34, 35 and Sonnet 60.

Did space permit we would give examples of Bacon's distinctively used words of the Sonnet, as, "lease," "augurs," "incertainties," "insults o'er," as we have them at hand. In this Sonnet, "thou" should be I. It is one of the cover word pronouns, and refers to the author himself, and in this, falls under our 7th Division of the Sonnets. In the open, it should stand, "And I in this shall find my monument," &c.

But again, the author of this Sonnet alludes to himself as "the mortal moon." Dr. Rawley, Bacon's Chaplain, and who had the nearest view of him, says: "It may seem the moon had some principal place in the figure of his nativity; for the moon was never in her passion, or eclipsed, but he was surprised with a sudden fit of fainting; and that, though he observed not nor took any previous knowledge of the eclipse thereof; and as soon as the eclipse ceased, he was restored to his former strength again." "Phil. Works," Vol. 1 p. 17. As to "eclipse" and the words "the figure of his nativity" see, please, Sonnet 60.

But this subject of the moon, "mortal moon;" has a deeper reach, reader. It lies deep in Bacon's distinctive views on astronomy as well as philosophy, as we will show later. He was aware that he possessed unusual mental gifts. He believed himself possessed of the first rudiment—note it—of self-sustained flame. The earth he believed pendant, and without motion, save in its own body; contrary to the views of his, or our own day. Flame in nature he believed first self-sustained, though weak, at the height or body of the moon; where it first begins to roll itself into globes; while at the sun, flame is on her throne. He says, below the moon, flame is flickering and halting with the fall, and requires to be fed. He believed the moon to be the last sediment of earthly, and the first rudiment of heavenly, or self-sustained flame; and himself to be of that sediment and first rudiment; and so, the "mortal moon" of the Sonnet. We have particularized these distinctive views as they are wrought into every phase of the writings here called under review, Milton not excepted.

Note them, please, as bearing upon the question of his wonderful authorship. Throughout these writings we have his ever used words "flame" and "inflame" as applied to mind. He says, "Mind is the divine fire." In the Plays we have, "the flame of love," the "heat and flame of thy distemper," "love's hot fire," "the wicked fire of lust," "the blaze of youth," and, "up with inflaming wrath." His Chaplain, Dr. Rawley, of his mental gifts says: "I have been induced to think, that if there were a beam of knowledge derived from God upon any man in these modern times, it was upon him. For though he was a great reader of books, yet he had not his knowledge from books, but from some grounds and notions from within himself." "Phil. Works," Vol. 1, p. 2.

The mentioned misplaced paper which concerns his "Formula," opens thus: "Believing that I was born for the service of mankind, and regarding the care of the commonwealth as a kind of common property which like the air and the water belongs to everybody, I set myself to consider in what way mankind might be best served, and what service I was myself best fitted by nature to perform."

Further on, touching his own gifts, he says, "For myself, I found that I was fitted for nothing so well as for the study of Truth; as having a mind nimble and versatile enough to catch the resemblances of things (which is the chief point), and at the same time steady enough to fix and distinguish their subtler differences; as being gifted by nature with desire to seek, patience to doubt, fondness to meditate, slowness to assert, readiness to reconsider, carefulness to dispose and set in order; and as being a man that neither affects what is new nor admires what is old, and that hates every kind of imposture. So I thought my nature had a kind of familiarity and relationship with Truth." "Bacon's Letters," Vol. 3 p. 84. As to "truth" see Sonnet 101.

This paper surely should be read in full. More of himself is said in it than will be found in all the rest of his attributed writings. He in it provides for the publication of his writings to posterity, reserving, however, the "Formula." See Chapter 3. p. 66 and 67.

Subsequent to his fall Bacon speaks of "the good pens that forsake me not." He says: "And since I have lost much time with this age, I would be glad as God shall give me leave, to recover it with posterity." Speaking of his great system, as a whole, he says: "For the great business God conduct it well." Again he says: "I must confess my desire to be, that my writings should not court the present time or some few places in such sort as might make them either less general to persons or less permanent in future ages." He says: "And if I should hereafter have leisure to write upon government the work will probably either be posthumous or abortive."

In his great posterity drama, he purposed to instruct "the actors themselves." Subsequent to his fall as already stated he in a letter to Gondomar says: "But for myself, my age, my fortune, yea my Genius, to which I have hitherto done but scant justice, calls me now to retire from the stage of civil action and betake myself to letters, and to the instruction of the actors themselves, and the service of Posterity. In this it may be I shall find honor, and I shall pass my days, as it were in the entrance halls of a better life." "Bacon's Letters," Vol. 7, p. 285. These are Francis Bacon's own words, not ours, reader.

To the time of his fall, he had carried his life labors double; in the open, in part, towards his own day; and in the dark towards posterity, or his Posthumous Pocket on which he ever had his eye. This Pocket, we say, consisted of "the cabinets, boxes, and presses" named in his last will, dated December 19th, 1625. He says in it, they are "that durable part of my memory."

His new flooring of knowledge for posterity he frames now upon a new basis. He retailors portions of his first period and he sits, as his own critic, upon the rest.

His ideational scope is indicated in the words wherein he says, "Knowledge is the image of existence." He could yield that image in words more accurately and elegantly, reader, than could any other son of Adam.

He was the swift catcher and easy delineator of all human motives; and he painted with unerring ornament of speech. His Shakespeare Plays were designed to untangle the passions and place them in the open. This he believed the beginning and business of all true instruction. With his views the true instructor must come ever upon the plane, mental and moral, of him he would instruct. Thus only can attention be gained and retained. This must be had, or reform abandoned. And so in the trap, or web of entertainment, must the instructed be caught and held firm to the instructor's art.

This is the pivotal point in both of Bacon's literary periods. Already in our Introduction we have called attention to Bacon's views as to the value of the knowledge of evil, to him who would be the true instructor. And so in his "Meditationes Sacrae" he says:

"To a man of perverse and corrupt judgment all instruction or persuasion is fruitless and contemptible which begins not with discovery and laying open of the distemper and ill complexion of the mind which is to be recured: as a plaster is unseasonably applied before the wound be searched. For men of corrupt understanding, that have lost all sound discerning of good and evil, come possessed with this prejudicate opinion, that they think all honesty and goodness proceedeth out of a simplicity of manners, and a kind of want of experience and unacquaintance with the affairs of the world. Therefore except they may perceive those things which are in their hearts, that is to say their own corrupt principles and the deepest reaches of their cunning and rottenness, to be thoroughly sounded and known to him that goes about to persuade with them, they make but a play of the words of wisdom. Therefore it behoveth him which aspireth to a goodness not retired or particular to himself, but a fructifying and begetting goodness, which should draw on others, to know those points which he called in the Revelation *the deeps of Satan;* that he may speak with authority and true insinuation. Hence is the precept: *Try all things, and hold fast that which is good;* which induceth a discerning election out of an examination whence nothing at all is excluded. Out of the same fountain ariseth that direction: *Be you wise as Serpents, and innocent as Doves.* There are neither teeth nor stings, nor venom, nor wreaths and folds of serpents, which ought not to be all known, and as far as examination doth lead, tried; neither let any man here fear infection or pollution; for the sun entereth into sinks and is not defiled. Neither let any man think that herein he tempteth God; for his diligence and generality of examination is commanded; and *God is sufficient to preserve you immaculate and pure.*" "Bacon's Literary Works" by Spedding, Vol. 2, p. 244. And so, the bed-rock design in both literary periods of this vast reformer, Bacon, is here graphically portrayed.

He taught both the hovel, and the palace, and he framed his speech for each. His Plays were but his "wood notes." They represent the world, and were warbled wild to be elsewhere expanded into a new literary age. They are patterns for the ages yet to be. Passions, prejudices, motives are here opened to the intellect. Entertainment makes it ever attentive and retentive. Knowledge,—light,—he believed to be our only true fence against evil.

In his Posthumous Pocket labors, known as the Voyages and Stories of Defoe, we have the same object in view as in the Plays; though falling into a slower measure. See, please, our "Defoe Period," p. 31 to 40. In them is found that graphic narrational style seen in his "New Atlantis."

The web of entertainment must 'ever catch and hold the attention. His "Pilgrim's Progress" labors will catch and hold the multitude, while school divinity entertains but few.

So distinctive now in our quotation, is Bacon's word "recured," and his expression "the complexion of the mind," that we halt to note them. "Complexion," as applied to mind, is distinctive, is Baconian. Note "complexion of the mind," in many examples, in the plays. See "recured" in Bacon's identical sense of use in Sonnet 45 and later in Milton. This Sonnet with Sonnet 146 presents the basis of Bacon's mental philosophy. Would that we might stay to elaborate it. But this threadline treatise is to be no loitering, but a march.

Touching the views as to Love and Lust, in this literature, and their effects, see Sonnet 116 and 129. In the "Venus and Adonis" we have:

> "Love comforteth like sunshine after rain,
> But lust's effect is tempest after sun;
> Love's gentle spring doth always fresh remain,
> Lust's winter comes ere summer half be done;
> Love surfeits not, lust like a glutton dies;
> Love is all truth, lust full of forged lies."

Bacon says: "Nuptial love maketh mankind; friendly love perfecteth it; but wanton love corrupteth and embaseth it." See here our "Defoe Period" p. 128 to 144.

Bacon's ability to throw his composition, poetry or prose, into almost any kind of structure and so carry it, rendered him a literary marvel. His mental physiognomy reveals itself best, however, in his vocabulary, distinctive idioms, and world scope. He used not the words of the metaphysician. In obedience to his own tabular method, his words follow ever the line of physics. The words applied to matter, he applies equally to mind. This was the law of his words throughout. He says: "It is the perfect law of the inquiry of truth, that there be nothing in the globe of matter, that has not its parallel in the globe of crystal or the understanding." Again

HIS POSTHUMOUS POCKET LABORS 117

he says: "When true physics have been discovered there will be no metaphysics."

This law of his words will be found throughout his Shakespeare and in all the parts or "pen-names" here called under review, reader.

His "New Atlantis," now begins abruptly as if the broken off or concluding part of some more extended composition. It opens thus:

"We sailed from Peru (where we had continued by the space of one whole year), for China and Japan, by the South Sea; taking with us victuals for twelve months; and had good winds from the east, though soft and weak, for five months' space and more. But then the wind came about, and settled in the west for many days, so as we could make little or no way, and were sometimes in purpose to turn back. But then again there arose strong and great winds from the south, with a point east: which carried us up (for all that we could do) towards the north: by which time our victuals failed us, though we had made good spare of them. So that finding ourselves in the midst of the greatest wilderness of waters in the world, without victuals, we gave ourselves for lost men, and prepared for death. Yet we did lift up our hearts and voices to God above, who *showeth His wonders in the deep;* beseeching him of his mercy, that as in the beginning he discovered the face of the deep, and brought forth dry land, so he would now discover land to us, that we might not perish. And it came to pass that the next day about evening, we saw within a kenning before us, toward the north, as it were thick clouds, which did put us in some hope of land; knowing how that part of the South Sea was utterly unknown; and might have islands or continents, that hitherto were not come to light." "Phil. Works," Vol. 3, p. 129. Already we have touched the "South Sea" and Bacon's secret, thwarted revenue scheme; and the later attempt by Harley to reinact it. It was said to be "his masterpiece." See here our "Defoe Period," p. 384 to 388.

The "New Atlantis" will be found at one in style and structure generally with the narrational portions of the Defoe literature, of a hundred years later. Let its every feature be carefully contrasted with "Robinson Crusoe;" that semblance of artlessness which is the perfection of art. In our "Defoe Period" we have devoted fourteen full pages to Bacon's range of knowledge, vocabulary, and distinctive expressions, to be found in Crusoe. See p. 388 to 402, then 17, 27, 28 and 64. To encourage colonization was the prominent feature in many of the stories. Crusoe is a distinct platform for new beginnings. See Bacon on Colonization. It was the most notable feature in the reign of James the 1st. Crusoe was to be the beginning of the new narrational method, wherein facts were to be made royal. See our "Defoe Period," p. 64. And on p. 317 Bacon as late as 1622 says he purposes to write "some patterns of natural story." He represents truth as an island. Note the island in "Crusoe," in the "New Atlantis," and in "The Tempest." In "The Tempest," the rabble, personated by Caliban, as the body of the times, is upon his island and claims, "to be the lord on't." They would sow it with "nettle-seed."

Yet the "New Atlantis" will be found to be the only piece of narrational composition with which Francis Bacon's name is now associated. So his "Holy War" is the only piece now attributed to him wherein he has attempted to handle a subject by way of dialogue. Yet note, reader, that they each are masterpieces in their line. The "Holy War" will show Bacon could carry a subject in dialogue with as much grace and ease as in his Shakespeare plays. He carried it some twenty pages in the open; far enough to lay the platform for such a war, we say: and then broke it off for the Bunyan work, by the same title. He was the great teacher, who retired, not his thoughts, nor his body, like the Monks, but who hooded his personality from portions of his writings leaving them thus to time.

Reader, when you have carefully analyzed the life, and life doings, of this great genius, you will have wrought into the deepest posterity project which time presents. You will find Macaulay's words touching this literary Sampson not over-wrought wherein he says: "He had an amplitude of comprehension which was never yet vouchsafed to any other human being." He was, indeed, a mystery to himself, as we shall later see from his own words in the "Cypher Work."

Among other things you will find the vocabulary of Sonnets, plays, and of all the herein claimed Posthumous Pocket labors to be, in identity, Bacon's vocabulary; and the encyclopedic range of knowledge throughout his range. Though chewed and re-chewed, spread and re-spread, it is all Baconian paste. So in Sonnet 76 "as the sun is daily new and old, so is my love still telling what is told."

While possessed of these wide gifts, still, Bacon had broken from the fold of literary domination. The universities and all of the seats of learning of his own day were held hide-bound to Aristotle, the then literary dictator. Though lauding his gifts, Bacon still called him "a straggler from experience," and left the fold.

How was Bacon now to stem prejudices as well from the universities and pulpits, as elsewhere, and gain attention? How was his own literary wonder, his New Age, to take root? Hope from his own day there was none. An untried art must now be devised to open the way; to open the intellect, and break the stubborn back of prejudices and literary domination; and as well from Rome as elsewhere. This was his "almost new feature in the intellectual world," touched later.

Human prejudices! Where, O reader, can be found a more hateful devil to human progress? As we lower our prejudices we ever beat the devil, and see clearer.

The new Art became known as the Club system of the Defoe period. They, for a time at least, were to be the new seats of learning; and his "Grubean Sages," his "Classic Authors in Wood," were to be their true instructors. Into these new seats of learning was to be poured a varied literary entertainment suited to the capacities of all. We have here again the trap or web of entertainment for opening the human intellect. It was ever the dark side method of this great genius. This system will later be called to relation with his "Tale of a Tub" addressed to posterity.

Touching this new or Club system, we from his "Grubean Sage," Addison, Bohn's edition, Vol. 2, p. 253 quote thus:

"The mind that lies fallow but a single day, sprouts up in follies that are only to be killed by a constant and assiduous culture. It was said of Socrates that he brought Philosophy down from heaven, to inhabit among men; and I shall be ambitious to have it said of me, that I have brought Philosophy out of closets and libraries, schools and colleges, to dwell in clubs and assemblies, at tea-tables and in coffee-houses." The Essay should be read in full, and in connection with chapter 15, Vol. 5 of "Knights' History of England."

These Clubs became now the literary feeding booths for the English people, concerning matters of State, theology, mythology, philosophy, and every phase of human thinking and the weedings thereof. What the stage had been to the first literary period, the Clubs were now to the second. They were the forum.

With Observer, Spectator, Tatler, Guardian, and other "Grubean Sage" works we would gladly open this feature of our subject, did space permit. Let some one of our good Sir Knights place this Addison Essay and its design into due relation, as an introductory opening to the Club system. To help him forward a little in it, we give Francis Bacon's own words thus:

"You are right in supposing that my great desire is to draw the sciences out of their hiding-places into the light. For indeed to write at leisure that which is to be read at leisure matters little; but to bring about the better ordering of man's life and business, with all its troubles and difficulties, by the help of sound and true contemplations,—this is the thing I am at. How great an enterprise in this kind I am attempting, and with what small helps, you will learn perhaps hereafter."

A little further on in it he says, "Surely I think no man could ever more truly say of himself with the Psalm than I can, 'My soul hath been a stranger in her pilgrimage.' So I seem to have my conversation among the ancients more than among these with whom I live."

"Bacon's Letters," Vol. 4, p. 147. Touching the universities Bacon says: "But alas, they learn nothing there but to believe; first to believe that others know that which they know not; and after that themselves know that which they know not." "Bacon's Letters," Vol. 1, p. 125. And see p. 82 and 86 as to papal influences over them; also "Literary Works," Vol. 1, p. 313 to 318. Much might be quoted here did space permit.

Unless our claim be true, reader, where now are those writings wherein Francis Bacon, and as "almost a new feature in the intellectual world," played "the nurse both with his own thoughts and those of others?" See please our "Defoe Period," p. 38 and 39.

Let now Bacon's undated letter, from which our former quotation comes, be joined here with one, the date of which has concededly been tampered with. And why tampered with? We, without hesitation say, it was written after Bacon's fall; and not to Bodley, as claimed. Few of his misplaced papers have more befogged his work. We give it in full, thus:

"I think no man may more truly say with the Psalm *Multum incola fuit anima mea*, than myself. For I do confess, since I was of any understanding, my mind hath in effect been absent from that I have done; and in absence are many errors which I do willingly acknowledge; and amongst the rest this great one that led the rest; that knowing myself by inward calling to be fitter to hold a book than to play a part, I have led my life in civil causes; for which I was not very fit by nature, and more unfit by the preoccupation of my mind. Therefore calling myself home, I have now for a time enjoyed myself; whereof likewise I desire to make the world partaker. My labours (if I may so term that which was the comfort of my other labours) I have dedicated to the King; desirous, if there be any good in them, it may be as the fat of a sacrifice, incensed to his honour: and the second copy I have sent unto you, not only in good affection, but in a kind of congruity, in regard of your great and rare desert of learning. For books are the shrines where the Saint is, or is believed to be: and you having built an Ark to save learning from deluge, deserve propriety in any new instrument or engine, whereby learning should be improved or advanced. "Bacon's Letters," Vol. 3, p. 253. In a foot-note Vol. 4, p. 64, Mr. Spedding tells us the date of this letter 1607 has been tampered with. He says: "I find that this date (though probably correct) is a modern addition, inferred probably from the date of Bodley's answer."

The letter from which the first quotation comes is addressed "To Casaubon." A foot-note tells us it had "No signature, date, docket or address." Addressing it to Casaubon, as addressing this to Bodley, was the result of a mere inference, to say no worse of it. This letter we say was written after Bacon's fall.

Let its words to the King "as the fat of a sacrifice," be called to relation with Sonnet 125 where we have "But mutual render only me for thee." Contrast then the first half of this letter, reader, with Sonnet 111 and bow yourself out of this investigation, if you find not reasons for our claim. As to the "Calling myself home" see Sonnet 100. As to "For books are the shrines," we may touch this later.

Improper headings, misplacings for want of dates, as well as tampering with Bacon's manuscripts, should receive greater attention than has yet been given them. What motive, see p. 61, could have induced Toby

Mathews to his extensive tamperings with Bacon's letters addressed to him, as shown by Mr. Spedding? See in this "Bacon's Letters," Vol. 7, p. 336 to 348 and 378. Note Bacon's undated letter to Mathews, after he had turned Catholic. Followed it the Somerset trial? See the letter, please, Vol. 4, p. 10. Note its words "as another hell above the ground." As an example of this tampering, we in a foot-note, page 364 have, "The letter had been dated 21 originally. But the 1 had been turned into 7 afterwards, and with a paler ink. The 1621 should also have been changed to 1622." Mr. Spedding's date 1622 is but assumed, and so this important letter is twice befogged, reader. See, please, in this connection Bacon's letter, Vol. 3, p. 216. Let these two letters be then called to relation with Bacon's secret revenue scheme, and the business of the already mentioned Referees.

We return here to the new Art, the new seats of learning, the clubs and coffee-houses. The coffee-house came somewhat earlier than the clubs. Macaulay of it says, "It was a political institution, and every man of the upper and middle class went daily to his coffee-house to learn the news and to discuss it."

The new seats of learning were designed to entertain the mind, to open it; to build it; to weed its prejudices. Here, as in his Shakespeare, Bacon made characters distinctive. The multiplicity of letters to, and the letters between the Sages, were but part of the scheme, and they were designed largely to give occasion for the articles themselves, "the lucubrations." They each and all came from that "amplitude of comprehension which was never yet vouchsafed to any other human being." These, then, were the Clubs, with which

HIS POSTHUMOUS POCKET LABORS 125

Francis Bacon was to down, beat back, or neutralize literary and ecclesiastic domination of the mind; to the end that it might once more be open and free to something new. This Club system, "this instruction of the world in single papers," reader, was that "almost a new feature in the intellectual world" wherein Bacon played the nurse as well with his own thoughts as those of others. See in this our "Defoe Period," p. 38 to 40; and p. 457 and notes. In his "Addision" Vol. 4, p. 172 he opens his paper thus: "The first who undertook to instruct the world in single papers, was Isaac Bickerstaff of famous memory." It should be read in full. Swift also was Bickerstaff.

The knowledge of the Club writers was one in scope, and that scope Bacon's. What one knew, they all knew, to its minutest detail. They were each and all expert in ancient learning. In other words, Bacon was thus expert. And as in Sonnet 68 "To show false Art what beauty was of yore." The Sages were all mythologists, all theologians, all statemen, all philosophers, all astronomers, all poets. Each had the same vocabulary and that Bacon's of a hundred years earlier. Let this be disproved, reader; you may then flout our claim. Not only the words, but a distinctive and unusual use of common words prevails throughout. To instance; all make use of the word "fellows." We do not, however, as did Bacon, say, "heat and light are fellows in many effects," or, as in Addison, "the features of his face were not fellows," or, as in Defoe, "the two shoes that came to shore were not fellows."

It should likewise be remembered that in some of the manuscripts, chasms were left for insertions to conform them to the time. Some of them again have extensive unauthorized interpolations. See our "Defoe Period," in this, p. 440 to 446, also p. 40 and 420. Again, the subjects handled in these papers are chiefly such as to make them of interest at any historic period, and they were studiously and adroitly handled to that end. So from the "Grubean Sage" Addison Vol. 3, p. 435 we have: "Most of the papers I give the public are written on subjects that never vary, but are for ever fixt and immutable. Of this kind are all my more serious essays and discourses; but there is another sort of speculations, which I consider as occasional papers, that take their rise from the folly, extravagance, and caprice of the present age. For I look upon myself as one set to watch the manners and behaviour of my countrymen and contemporaries, and to mark down every absurd fashion, ridiculous custom, or affected form of speech, that makes its appearance in the world, during the course of these my speculations." From the Sage, Swift, we quote thus: "In all my writings I have had constant regard to this great end, not to suit and apply them to particular occasions and circumstances of time, of place, or of person, but calculate them for universal nature and mankind in general." See Bacon's own words in this, p. 112. Let the reader have a careful eye to this point in the general scope of these writings. Also see Chapter 15, Vol. 5, "Knight's History of England."

The inundation of this literature began its career under the leadership of Sir Robert Harley. In our "Defoe Period," p. 402 to 447 we present both Harley and Defoe, and very carefully Defoe, whose true name was Foe, he being the son of James Foe. Daniel, save by his initials, never subscribed any portion of the writings now attributed to him. The initials were not used prior to his arrest in 1703. He was a liveryman in London at the age of 27. Chalmers, in closing his life of Defoe, having examined Stationers Hall, says: "I was surprised and disappointed to find so few of Defoe's writings entered as property, and his name never mentioned as an author or a man."

Harley while prisoner in the Tower was accredited with the authorship of the first volume of Crusoe. While Defoe, Addison, Swift, Pope and others were the dial-plate; still, Harley was the financial or real movement in playing out Bacon's posterity drama, now known as the English Augustan Age. Did he play it, reader, for the author's, or boggle it for his own ends?

We are aware that the views here presented must of necessity require time to ripen. Should the reader incline to the views already advanced, let him take no prejudice now to that which is to follow; as later it will return with redoubled light over the field already trod. Let him as romance receive it until it ripen into fact, as it surely will. We cautiously, touched it in our "Defoe Period" p. 182 to 186. We here and now, under better light, affirm it, thus:

When Francis Bacon was driven by the King's physician to Highgate on the morning of April 2nd, 1626, we say he was not en route for death at the Earl of Arundel's house, as now generally supposed; but rather was upon his departure from the realm of England to a secret retreat at the Hague, or in Germany, where he now rested his hopes for the Protestant cause. Entertained he such secret design when making his last will some four months earlier? Facts at times are stranger than fiction, reader. Note the significant words in the will wherein he says: "For my name and memory, I leave it to men's charitable speeches, and to foreign nations and the next ages." He certainly had received strange treatment in his own. His wealth had been taken. Even York House, which he supposed saved from the first wreck, he was compelled to yield up at Buckingham's dictation. Had Buckingham secret designs on Bacon's life, known to King Charles, when driven by his physician to Highgate? See our "Defoe Period," p. 184 and 185. See also the undated papers concerning some secret business between Buckingham, Bacon and Highgate. "Bacon's Letters," Vol. 7, p. 346 to 348, and 354 and 5. Buckingham's impeachment began a little later in the Parliament which convened February 6th, 1626. See p. 95.

If Bacon's death had really occurred at this time at the Earl of Arundel's house near Highgate; where were his funeral rites performed? Who pronounced the funeral oration of this noted genius? And what noblemen attended the last sad rites? Was Arundel himself there? Was Dr. Rawley there? England has here no voice.

She says for fourteen months, though leaving a will dated December 19th, 1625 no one assumed control of his estate; and later assumed only by creditors, the executors declining to act. Mr. Spedding informs us his manuscripts were sent to the Hague. And why to the Hague? See "Phil. Works," Vol. 3, p. 3 to 10. "Bacon's Letters," Vol. 1, p. 16, Vol. 2, p. 2 and 3. The will itself will be found in Vol. 7, p. 539.

In the will Bacon refers to the "cabinets, boxes and presses" as "that durable part of my memory, which consisteth in my works and writings."

HIS POSTHUMOUS POCKET LABORS 129

We here arrive at the Posthumous Pocket labors of Sir Francis Bacon to this time evolved. Later, in the Defoe period they, with others, gave Robert Harley place and fame. How the manuscripts came to his hands must be told later. Let some good St. Alban Knight here lend aid. Bacon's literary retinue, in his first period, were his "pen-names," so, in his second, his "Grubean Sages," Addison, Defoe, Swift and others were the retinue or retainers of Sir Robert Harley, and they rendered him both service and honor. Lee, Defoe's biographer, says of Harley "we admire the discernment and tact of the minister who could engage, in support of his policy the pens of such man as Addison, Swift, Defoe, Steele, Arbuthnot, Prior, and Davenant; though some of them were opposed to each other, personally and politically."

"Henslow's Diary" in the first period, concerns managers, assistants, not writers, though doubtless thought to be so, by the ignorant tool Henslow, who permitted them as they would to make entries in it. Among the "pen-names" or "Sages" of Bacon's second period, Milton will be found chief, reader.

Though in concealment, Bacon remained long at labor. He was ever a careful student of both methods, and medicines, to preserve longevity. We claim for him an advanced age, extending until after the trial and execution of Charles the 1st in 1649, until which time Bacon's hopes failed not of becoming England's rightful Sovereign.

In later pages we will make it clear from Mrs. Gallup's own work, that she has, as yet, but discovered the cyphers which concern Bacon's first literary period. The great cypher over all, "The Capital Letter Cypher," or

Bacon's great "Alphabet of Nature," remains as yet undiscovered.

We would have the reader return with us here to the subject of cypher writing; and to the distinctive uncalled for use of capital letters; as set out in all of the "Newly Discovered Defoe Papers." See our "Defoe Period," p. 447 to 520. The Addison article on the subject of capital letters will be found in Bohn's edition Vol. 3, p. 102 to 105. It ends thus: "This instance will, I hope, convince my readers, that there may be a great deal of fine writing in the capital letters which bring up the rear of my paper, and give them some satisfaction in that particular. But as for the full explication of these matters, I must refer them to time, which discovers all things." See our "Defoe Period," p. 456 to 460.

The reader should turn now to his "Sartor Resartus," or, tailor re-tailored; that waif, that left-over from Bacon's Posthumous Pocket, that work of durance, that master wheel in the use of the mentioned capital letters. It, with marvelous concentration, covers, we say, both of Francis Bacon's literary periods. It will be touched to relation in Chapter 5. How it; how the "Hero Worship," the "Past and Present," and "Cromwell's Letters and Speeches" came to the hands of Thomas Carlyle we know not; but unhesitatingly say to the reader that they were not products of Carlyle's pen, save interpolations, many of which they surely contain. The entire Chapter on Cromwell and Napoleon in the "Hero Worship," save the opening pages, is by another, a weaker, and an entirely different hand. This is equally true of the Chapter on "The Hero As a Man of Letters;" so far as it treats of Rousseau and Burns. The interpolated portions treating of Napoleon, Rosseau, and Burns, were evidently designed to bring down or link the writings to a later date, thus averting thoughts of earlier authorship.

While claiming to be editor of "Cromwell's Letters and Speeches," the interpolator fails wholly to conceive the business and real design of the Cromwell party; the Independents. The Essay fails to comprehend the struggle of the times. It regards Cromwell and his party as Puritans which they surely were not. In it he speaks of the "deep-hearted Calvinistic Cromwell." This belies both the Independents and their leader—their Joshua. The Independents for power, and the end they sought, did covertly work with, and make use of them; but surely were not of them. Many readers have failed to note this. Again, the Essay is but a weak imitation of the master hand. While borrowing some of his words and phrases, it still gives but a lame pace to many unfound in his diction. Let this weak Essay on Cromwell be contrasted, for instance, with the first Essay or lecture on "The Hero As Divinity;" or with the editorial work itself on the "Letters and Speeches." The business of an editor here, as in the "Sartor Resartus," is but part of the scheme or method of production, reader. There is, save interpolations, but the one hand in these writings. We say these Carlyle works were surely waifs, were left-overs, from the Bacon budget. No careful student, after investigation, dare affirm Carlyle's authorship of them. We have not as yet called "The French Revolution" under review. It will probably be found but a chopped, a garbled work. That Bacon intended to begin the publication of his writings in France, see please our "Defoe Period," p. 222.

This brings us to the times, and doings, of that greatly misunderstood man, Oliver Cromwell. As Aaron was secretary and mouth-piece to Moses; so Francis Bacon became covert secretary and mouth-piece to Cromwell, and to that secret knot of sturdy Englishmen including Rawley, John Milton and others; who, had it been possible, would have placed him as Francis 1st of England.

To the public, in the conflict of parties, their true aims were covered; were cloaked. They were staunch supporters of the English church, and in party came to be known as the Independents. They were but movers of factions. They sought to place the church upon its true ancient foundation; weeded, as Bacon puts it, "from Henry the 8ths' confusion." He desired to return it to its attitude in the second century. The swelling power of the Bishops they thought not consistent with the meek and lowly teachings of the Word. Throughout the plays, where church influences come in question, note the domination by Bishop or Archbishop over both King and counsel. And note power, fished by them from below; from the "seconds". As to Bishops and their power see, please, "Bacon's Letters," Vol. 3, p. 108, 114. And on page 265 we have "A case forlorn, that Romish subtlety should underprop English formality."

In Vol. 1, p. 17 of his Milton's prose works, Bohn's edition, he defines the position of the Independents, thus: "They that we call independents, are only such as hold that no classis or synods have a superiority over any particular church, and that therefore they ought all to be plucked up by the roots, as branches, or rather as the very trunk, of hierarchy itself." And see p, 260. In Vol. 2, p. 362 to 509 their views on Bishops and church government are most critically analyzed and defined. Few, we think, are familiar with these wonderful prose writings. Until recently we were among that number. We do not believe clearer views on both ecclesiastic and popular rights can anywhere be found in literature. Here Bacon was surely living his "second life on second head," as stated in Sonnet 68. He was rechewing for posterity his first literary period and weeding from it the now offensive doctrine of the divine right of kings entertained to the time of his fall; and graphically set out in his government model, later to be called under review and now known as the "Leviathan."

With Presbyterians, Puritan dissenters, and Papists; the Independents bore no sympathy. To Presbyterians they were sharply opposed; believing their root in church government would end in Papal power. See, please, "Carlyle's Cromwell," Everyman's Library edition, Vol. 1, p. 211. See this most graphically portrayed in Addison, Bohn's edition, Vol. 2, p. 205 to 210. The same views find expression in the "Tale of a Tub." See in this our "Defoe Period" p. 574 and 584. Here Papists and Calvin, as "Knocking Jack of the North," are presented thus: "The frenzy and the spleen of both having the same foundation, we may look upon them as two pair of compasses, equally extended, and the fixed foot of each remaining in the same centre, which, though moving contrary ways at first, will be sure to encounter somewhere or other in the circumference." Note now, reader, how unjustly Carlyle, by interpolations, befogs this literature. He seeks to throw the value of Luther's reform to Calvin, or the Presbyterians. See "Hero Worship" lecture 4; Everyman's

Library edition, p. 372 and 3; and later choppings. Thus these writings, and the aims of the Independents are woefully belied. The Milton prose writings will fully show this.

Cromwell was but the vigorous outward—the dial-plate—of a most secret political movement in England to place Francis Bacon upon the English throne; and the English church upon its true ancient foundation. This was the mission. This, at bottom, was the spur to Bacon's endeavors. A lingering faith remained with him, that he would ultimately be crowned; and so reap the credit of his own vast labors.

In 1622, and so following his fall, he produced that adroitly written dialogue, entitled, "The Holy War." He carried it some twenty pages, and far enough to lay a true model or platform to justify such a war, and says: "Great matters (especially if they be religious) have (many times) small beginnings; and the platform may draw on the building." This model, we say, he broke off or discontinued for the Bunyan work, by the same title. It will be found in his "Literary Works" by Spedding, Vol. 2, p. 17 to 37.

Let the reader now find entertainment in seeing Francis Bacon turn this model into narration; in his "Serious Reflections" of Crusoe. "Defoe Period," p. 373 to 388, then p. 347 to 373. In the "Cromwell Letters" we may find the same views expressed concerning the establishing of religion by the sword, as in the "Crusoe work." An offensive religious war may be justly waged only to break and destroy mental domination, in other words, to open the door to religion; but in no sense to establish creeds or systems.

This platform was to be used against the Turks and pirates of Tunis and Algiers. It was moved first by Bacon following the Somerset trial; while the King was yet in Scotland; and to be included in the then on foot Spanish alliance of Prince Charles with the infanta of Spain; and by some, thought, with a view to thwart that marriage. See in this our examination of the play of "The Tempest." "Defoe Period" p. 319, 346. See also "Bacon's Literary Works" by Spedding, Vol. 2, p. 3 to 7. He most surely was in the way. He had long stood athwart the ripening of the Catholic cause. See, please, "Bacon's Letters," Vol. 7, p. 368 to 371. In his own day and a little earlier the tenacious struggle was on.

We come now to a point most difficult for our critics to evade. Bacon himself says: "But after furnishing the understanding with the most surest helps and precautions, and having completed, by a rigorous levy, a complete host of divine works, nothing remains to be done but to attack philosophy itself." This he says at the very opening of his crowning work, the "New Organ." See our "Defoe Period," p. 67 to 95. See Spedding's translation. "Phil. Works," Vol. 4, p. 31.

Where now are the mentioned "divine works?" Among those on inspired divinity; we refer to his Bunyan's "Holy War," and his "Pilgrim's Progress." Those on natural theology will be found in the Defoe Works. The concluding lines of the poem ending the "Holy War" are in these words:

"I write not this of any ostentation;
Nor 'cause I seek of men their commendation;
I did it to keep them from such surmize,

As tempt them will my name to scandalize.
Witness my name, if Anagram'd to thee,
The letters make *Nu hony in a* B."

As to this ever used word "ostentation" in these writings we quote Bacon, thus: "In fame of learning the flight will be slow without some feathers of ostentation."

In the poem opening the "Holy War," we have:

"Nor do thou go to work without my Key;
(In mysteries men soon do lose their way.)"

As to the "Pilgrim's Progress" see our "Defoe Period," p. 460 to 463, and p. 67 to 71.

This great dream drama is said to be the finest specimen of well sustained allegory in any language; yet is said to be the work of an untaught rustic. It is the work of a Dark author excusing his method by an introductory poem. He in it says:

"My dark and cloudy words, they do but hold
  The truth, as cabinets inclose the gold."

Bacon made characters as distinctive, in this drama, as in his Shakespeare.

Its first paragraph opens by a "Den." The business of the work is to present the idols or errors of that "den," in other words, our inner state of heart, life, mind, &c.

The four idols, or errors of men, Bacon presents as the idols or errors of the Den, of the Tribe, of the Market, of the Theater; and discusses each at some length. Throughout his Shakespeare we find such expressions as these: "God ye good den," "God give ye good den," "God dig—you—den all!" For examples from the plays, see our "Defoe Period," p. 111. On page 67, note what Bacon says as to the "stock of observations" necessary to write in allegory or aphorisms. Bunyan? Ha! In this levy upon the mental energies, there must be first an involution, reader, before there can be an evolution. In the "Pilgrim's Progress," "the den," the inner life of man is for better retention, portrayed in characters, mental pictures, so to speak. The science of theology is portrayed in it. Its author, we say, wrote Milton, wrote the Defoe "History and Reality of Apparitions," wrote the Defoe "History of the Devil," reader.

The "Pilgrim's Progress" concerns the person, the individual life, and its government. The "Holy War" concerns the many, the public. "The den" in it, is treated as a fortress, with its outer walls, and called a Town, the "Town of Mansoul." Theology in it, as in Milton, is treated as a warfare with all of its weapons. Touching these "outward walls" of the soul, see Sonnet 146, where the soul is said to be "the centre of my sinful earth." "Outward walls," are called, its "fading mansion." As "rebel powers," they array the soul.

We return to the contending factions with which Cromwell and his party, the Independents, had to deal, yea, to move; which they ever did covertly to their own ends. Let "Knight's History of England" from 1642 till the execution of the King, Charles the 1st, in 1649, be here read with reflection and care.

The act which culminated in the King's execution will be found graphically set out by Bacon in his Milton's prose works, Bohn's edition, Vol. 2, p. 139 to 200. On page 1 to 48 his execution is fully justified in an article entitled "The Tenure of Kings and Magistrates." And on page 108 to 138 will be found presented a new form of government for England entitled "A Free Commonwealth." Bacon's "second life on second head" is here revealing itself, reader. We say he was surely its author.

The mentioned execution was resolved upon at a noted army "Prayer Meeting" in 1648. Described where? In "Cromwell's Letters and Speeches," Everyman's Library edition, Vol. 1, p. 254 to 260 and see page 215.

Was Carlyle its author? We unhesitatingly say he was not. Who was? Cromwell's secretary, the man who cast or recast his letters and speeches and was the editor of them. And still who? Francis Bacon himself, reader. Though in concealment, he was, we say, still living, and was the author of these writings. The letters are brief, covert, many of them having great subtlety, in managing the factions.

As the mouth-piece of Moses was Aaron; so Bacon as covert secretary, was behind Oliver Cromwell and his party, in its great secret struggle. Why then upon the execution of Charles, did not his adherents proclaim him King? To answer this, was the design of our recent reference to "Knight's History of England." In the face of contending factions then existing, and Bacon's advanced years, they dare not now disclose their hand, their long carried secret. It died with them.

And so, again, Bacon chose to leave his record to time and his Posthumous Pocket labors. Their inundation had not as yet begun. Extremity of romance? Yes, surely so, and yet true, reader! Bacon may now have thought as earlier he did, in the words which he put into the mouth of his favorite King Henry the 5th Act I, Sce. 2 where he says:

"Either our history shall, with full mouth,
  Speak freely of our acts; or else our grave,
  Like Turkish mute, shall have a tongueless mouth,
  Not worship'd with a waxen epitaph."

He, and his aims, were largely self-centered in this play. There was no English King more valued by Francis Bacon. The play was first in print, as we now have it, in the Folio of 1623. It is a kind of government model. It is a light to all rulers. It seeks to make manifest that all government rulers should possess an accurate knowledge of the deeps of Satan. To truly govern, rulers must know "the seconds." Note these in Sonnet 125. They must in other words know the strong holds, the haunts of vice, and how to weed them.

Bacon's views as to the value of an accurate knowledge of the depths of evil, in order to guard the good, have earlier been quoted p. 114. And see our "Defoe Period," p. 31 to 41. How in the play the King acquired his accurate knowledge of evil must be told of his youth as Prince Henry of Monmouth, in the play concerning his father, Henry the IV, where his seeming profligacy is presented as an art, in the study of those elements which he must later meet and control when he himself came to the throne. Bacon had been making a like study.

In dramatic form the plays may be said to present the history of England or the Tudor line to the days of Elizabeth. They throughout show that the best aims of both church and state, are dominated and thwarted by influences fished from "the seconds," from the slums. Here, as in his Milton, "the deeps of Satan" are portrayed.

This Monmouth King, in the play, is drawn to contrast with Alexander the Great, and with a portrayed design to possess France, and from thence to Constantinople and the Turks. In the "Sartor Resartus" Bohn's edition p. 282, to be used in this work, note "Monmouth Street, at the bottom of our own English ink-sea." And let it be drawn into close relation with this play. Bacon contrasts his own doings with those of Alexander and says: "I promise to myself a like fortune to that of Alexander the Great: and let no man tax me with vanity till he has heard the end." "Phil. Works," Vol. 4, p. 93.

His "Holy War" dialogue will show how he could handle a serious subject, wherein his chosen words must, of necessity, conform. If the reader will now see how he could likewise handle, by way of dialogue, a different and extremely literary and entertaining subject, let him turn to his Addison "Dialogues on Medals." Bohn's edition, Vol. 1, p. 255 to 356. We say to you, reader, Francis Bacon wrote these dialogues.

Medals, his "faithful registers," were the vat, so to speak, out of which Francis Bacon fished up, retailored, and restored, ancient fables to their true Hebrew roots, for his own use. Thus restored, he, in them, was "painted new," as stated in Sonnet 53. In these medals you may discover the wonderful assistance received by him in interpreting ancient fables, as set out in his "Wisdom Of The Ancients," and elsewhere, and spread throughout these writings. These medals were, we say, the "faithful registers" to which he refers in his "New Atlantis."

See our "Defoe Period," p. 543. From it, we quote thus: "This island (as appeareth by faithful registers of those times) had there fifteen hundred strong ships, of great content. Of all this there is with you sparing memory, or none; but we have large knowledge thereof." He elsewhere speaks of one "having obtained into his hands many registers and memorials out of the monastaries."

These "faithful registers" lent him great aid in deciphering the ancient poets, as well as the fables themselves. In some private notes wherein he calls himself to labor, we have "Discoursing scornfully of the philosophy of the Grecians with some better respect to the Egyptians, Persians, Chaldees, and the utmost antiquity and mysteries of the poets." "Bacon's Letters," Vol. 4, p. 64. "For I have taken all knowledge to be my providence" says Bacon.

His "Wisdom Of The Ancients" gives us chiefly those restored fables which he designed to use in connection with philosophy.

In his Addison, Bacon was his own critic. His critic's chair of the "De Augmentis" he, himself, occupied and said what he would of his own Posthumous Pocket labors, Milton included. See our "Defoe Period," p. 31 note 1. Addison, Vol. 3, p. 170 to 173. He himself was the true ancient critic. He was the restorer of ancient learning. "Defoe Period" p. 563 and 4. See here his Defoe paper on "Old Homer" where his "Alphabet of Nature," his "Capital Letter Cypher," is put to use. "Defoe Period" p. 517 to 521. Then see Addison Vol. 3 p. 45 to 49.

Having in Addison and Defoe touched but two of his "Grubean Sages"—his "Classic Authors in Wood"— we in his Swift's "Tale of a Tub" touch them all in a group. See in this our "Defoe Period," p. 587 to 605. It opens in these words, "To His Royal Highness Prince Posterity."

This Prince is asked to protect from the ravages of the tyrant Time the writings soon to come, or to be opened to him. The full group of "Grubean Sages" are on page 81, using Everyman's Library edition, referred to thus: "We, whom the world is pleased to honor with the title of modern authors, would never have been able to compass our great design of an everlasting remembrance and never-dying fame, if our endeavors had not been so highly serviceable to the general good of mankind. This, O Universe! is the adventurous attempt of me thy secretary."

And so "We" after all, was but "Me." I alone did the work, "O Universe!" As secretary to "Prince Posterity" I, Bacon, did it.

He describes this "secretary for the whole department of life" in his "Phil. Works," by Spedding, Vol. 5, p. 35. See Vol. 4, p. 278. Let this "Secretary" be kept in view throughout these writings. We have touched him already in connection with Cromwell and the Independents.

This great reformer here urges upon posterity protection for his vast literary carcass, his Posthumous Pocket labors—his New Golden Fleece. This sought protection from Time's tyranny is in full accord with his already considered Shakespeare Sonnets, reader.

All of Swift's writings, let it be distinctly remembered including "A Tale of a Tub," were first put forth anonymously. As to the writings of Addison we quote from the preface of Bohn's edition of his works thus: "The only works he left behind him for the public, are the Dialogues upon Medals, and the Treaties upon the Christian Religion." The last mentioned, we think originally designed as an introduction to the Milton prose work in two volumes entitled "Christian Doctrine" which was a waif, and was pigeon-holed for nearly a century and a half. See introduction to Bohn's edition. Already have we called attention to the anonymous writings of Defoe.

In both church and state Bacon followed the divine plan. He believed that God not only ruled the world in general; but that He, with a chosen people consisting of twelve tribes, set up a special government the doings of which were in general to be radiated upon society, He himself, being King; and that it continued unbroken to the time of Saul; since which kings have been His deputies on earth. This government he presents in his Milton's "Paradise Lost," beginning at page 260, using Everyman's Library edition, as we shall in this work.

His "New Atlantis" follows this model. Its design was the renovation, or new flooring, of all human learning. In other words he undertook to exercise "a providence" over all literature and learning.

Like the children of Israel, his "New Atlantis" consisted of twelve heads, and one concealed. See our "Defoe Period," in this p. 381 to 385. From its closing paragraph we have: "God bless thee, my son, and God bless this relation which I have made. I give thee leave to publish it for the good of other nations; for we here are in God's bosom, a land unknown." Were not his adherents members of it? How many became members subsequent to his fall? Did Cromwell belong? He was twenty-seven years of age at the time of Bacon's supposed death in 1626. He was a member of the Parliament that convened January 20th, 1629.

Again we say, as Aaron was secretary and mouthpiece to Moses; the only representative in God's government of the twelve tribes, so Bacon became secretary and secret adviser of Cromwell and the Independents during the great struggle that put Charles from the English throne. Note this "Lord chief *Secretary*" in "Bunyan's Holy War." As to the work of the Independents we from the preface of Vol. 1 of Milton's prose works quote thus: "For the first time perhaps, since the age of the apostles, Christianity was put in practice on a grand scale, by high-minded disinterested men, who sought in earnest to lay the foundations of an evangelical commonwealth, modelled in harmony with the precepts of the gospel, such as no other age or country ever yet aimed at." From the day of the restoration of the English monarchy a pseudo-literary domination has prevailed over this literature.

We now say to you, reader, that the letters and speeches of Oliver Cromwell were from Francis Bacon's own pen. We do not say Cromwell wrote no letters. But we do say, those that have come down to us, were cast, or recast by Bacon's own hand; and that he was their editor in the mentioned Carlyle work or waif. This was secret business for all concerned, John Milton included. Touching now this Chief Secretary; there were under secretaries; we from one of the Cromwell letters quote thus:

"Secretary Thurloe, once St. John's Secretary in Holland, has come now, ever since the Little-Parliament time, into decided action as Oliver's Secretary, or the State Secretary; one of the expertest Secretaries, in the

HIS POSTHUMOUS POCKET LABORS   145

real meaning of the word Secretary, any State or working King could have. He deals with all these Plots; it is part of his function, supervised by his Chief. Mr. John Milton, we all lament to know, has fallen blind in the Public Service, lives now in Bird-cage Walk, still doing a little when called upon; bating no jot of heart or hope. Mr. Milton's notion is, That this Protectorate of his Highness Oliver was a thing called for by the Necessities and the Everlasting Laws; and that his Highness ought now to quit himself like a Christian Hero in it, as in other smaller things he has been used to do." "Carlyle's Cromwell," Everyman's Library edition Vol. 3, p. 5. And see p. 105. St. John on p. 20 is said to be the political "dark-lantern."

Some of the letters and speeches are said to be of Oliver's mind, but admitted to be in the hand of another, in the hand of his secretary. Let the set form in opening all the letters, as well as their acute concentration and brevity be noted.

If now Bacon, as Oliver's secretary, framed these letters and speeches and was himself their editor, then must not our claim touching his morning drive to Highgate in 1626 page 127, be admitted, reader?

Then let critics to their work, remembering ever that some of these writings have been seriously tampered with. This of itself casts doubt on Carlyle's authorship. Even the introductory pages to the Letters and Speeches are much garbled. We say these writings came to Carlyle as waifs, as left-overs, from the Bacon Budget. Some of the Defoe and other writings under review are concededly waifs, and tampered with. See our "Defoe Period," p. 441 to 447. And see p. 31 and 40.

Bacon's secret return to England must have been prior, we think, to 1640. May his retreat possibly have been at Lady Place? See "Knight's History of England," Vol. 4 p. 357. There is evidence that during his absence, he visited Italy. Did space permit we would gladly place the "Cromwell Letters and Speeches" into Baconian relation, as to mythology, theology, vocabulary, and as to a distinctive and unusual use throughout of capital letters, though these are more sparingly used here, than in the "Sartor Resartus" later to be called under review. The reader must remember that we but outline or bound the field; leaving our good Sir Knights to lend here their aid. In fact the basis and business for our projected brotherhood, our St. Alban Knights, or, if preferred, Knights of Atlantis, rest here.

From the Carlyle waif the "Past and Present" we now touch the secret spring or point pushed at throughout the "Cromwell Letters and Speeches;"—to wit; "He is thy born king." From Everyman's Library edition of the work, p. 279, we quote thus:

"Not a May-game is this man's life; but a battle and a march, a warfare with principalities and powers. No idle promenade through fragrant orange-groves and green flowery spaces, waited on by the choral Muses and the rosy Hours: it is a stern pilgrimage through burning sandy solitudes, through regions of thick-ribbed ice. He walks among men; loves men, with inexpressible soft pity,—as they *cannot* love him: but his soul dwells in solitude, in the uttermost parts of Creation. In green oases by the palm-tree wells, he rests a space; but anon he has to journey forward, escorted by the Terrors and the Splendours, the Archdemons and Archangels. All Heaven, all Pandemonium are his escort.

The stars keen-glancing, from the Immensities, send tidings to him; the graves, silent with their dead, from the Eternities. Deep calls for him unto Deep.

"Thou, O World, how wilt thou secure thyself against this man? Thou canst not hire him by thy guineas; nor by thy gibbets and law-penalties restrain him. He eludes thee like a Spirit. Thou canst not forward him, thou canst not hinder him. Thy penalties, thy poverties, neglects, contumelies: behold, all these are good for him. Come to him as an enemy; turn from him as an unfriend; only do not this one thing,—infect him not with thy own delusion: the benign Genius, were it by very death, shall guard him against this!— What wilt thou do with him? He is above thee, like a god. Thou, in thy stupendous three-inch pattens, art under him. He is thy born king, thy conqueror and supreme lawgiver: not all the guineas and cannons, and leather and prunella, under the sky can save thee from him. Hardest thick-skinned Mammon-world, ruggedest Caliban shall obey him, or become not Caliban but a cramp. Oh, if in this man, whose eyes can flash Heaven's lightning, and make all Calibans into a cramp, there dwelt not, as the essence of his very being, a God's justice, human Nobleness, Veracity and Mercy,—I should tremble for the world. But his strength, let us rejoice to understand, is even this: The quantity of Justice, of Valour and Pity that is in him. To hypocrites and tailored quacks in high places his eyes are lightning; but they melt in dewy pity softer than a mother's to the downpressed, maltreated; in his heart, in his great thought, is a sanctuary for all the wretched. This world's improvement is forever sure. 'Man of genius?' Thou hast small notion, meseems, O Maecenas Twiddledee, of what a Man of Genius is. Read in thy New Testament and elsewhere,—if, with floods of mealy-mouthed inanity; with miserable froth-vortices of Cant now several centuries old, thy New Testament is not all bedimmed for thee. *Canst* thou read in thy New Testament at all? The Highest Man of Genius, knowest thou him; Godlike and a God to this hour? His crown a Crown of Thorns? Thou fool, with *thy* empty Godhoods, Apotheoses *edge-gilt;* the Crown of Thorns made into a poor jewel-room crown, fit for the head of blockheads; the bearing of the Cross changed to a riding in the Long-Acre Gig! Pause in thy mass-chantings, in thy litanyings, and Calmuck prayings by machinery; and pray, if noisily, at least in a more human manner. How with thy rubrics and dalmatics, and clothwebs and cobwebs, and with thy stupidities and grovelling baseheartedness, hast thou hidden the Holiest into all but invisibility!—

'Man of Genius:' O Maecenas Twiddledee, hast thou any notion what a Man of Genius is? Genius is 'the inspired gift of God.' It is the clearer presence of God Most High in a man. Dim, potential in all men; in this man it has become clear, actual. So says John Milton, who ought to be a judge; so answer him the Voices of all Ages and all Worlds."

The chapter from which the foregoing comes is entitled "The Gifted." It should be read in full. Its word "He," in the expression "He is thy born King," we understand to be but a pronoun cover word for the author himself, a method already found used in the Sonnets. In them Bacon's right to the throne has already been touched.

HIS POSTHUMOUS POCKET LABORS 149

If Carlyle be author of the feeble lecture on Cromwell in the "Hero Worship" then surely he was not author of the masterful Chapter from which our quotation comes; nor did he write that wonder, the "Sartor Resartus," soon to be reviewed. The word "forward" used in the foregoing will there be found ringing in the author's ears as an ever sounding sea. He there calls himself "The Son of Time." In some of the Swift writings he calls himself "the Great Unknown." Let the knowledge of mythology in the "Hero Worship," in Milton, in Shakespeare, be here called to Baconian relation. Returning to the "He is thy born King" we from the "Hero Worship," p. 345, quote thus:

"Here, I say, is an English King, whom no time or chance, Parliament or combination of Parliaments, can dethrone! This King Shakspeare, does not he shine, in crowned sovereignty, over us all, as the noblest, gentlest, yet strongest of rallying-signs; indestructible; really more valuable in that point of view than any other means of appliance whatsoever? We can fancy him as radiant aloft over all the Nations of Englishmen, a thousand years hence." By a chance Parliament it was that Bacon met his overthrow. He is here his own critic.

Again, p. 340 touching sorrow expressed in his Shakespeare Sonnets we have: "Yet I call Shakespeare greater than Dante, in that he fought truly, and did conquer. Doubt it not, he had his own sorrows: those *Sonnets* of his will even testify expressly in what deep waters he has waded, and swum struggling for his life."

And on p. 335 we have: "Of this Shakespeare of ours, perhaps the opinion one sometimes hears, a little idolatrously expressed is, in fact, the right one; I think the best judgment not of this country only, but of

Europe at large, is slowly pointing to the conclusion, that Shakespeare is the chief of all Poets hitherto; the greatest intellect who, in our recorded world, has left record of himself in the way of Literature. On the whole, I know not such a power of vision, such a faculty of thought, if we take all the characters of it, in any other man. Such a calmness of depth; placid joyous strength; all things imaged in that great soul of his so true and clear, as in a tranquil unfathomable sea! It has been said, that in the constructing of Shakespeare's Dramas there is, apart from all other 'faculties' as they are called, an understanding manifested, equal to that in Bacon's *Novum Organum*."

A like laudation of his Shake-speare, himself behind the mask, Bacon presents in his Ben Jonson poem already touched in earlier pages. See p. 80.

But would Francis Bacon thus openly as here make laudatory reference to his own name and work? This self-reference, self-laudation, see Sonnet 62, occurring in many places in these writings, and notably in his Addison, gives an opportunity to say here what we would concerning it. First, it tends to conceal the writer. Second, he in these writings chose to be his own critic, and say what he would of the works, overt or covert which he produced. No man knew better than Francis Bacon that, as to critics, the first makes the road, and the rest tread meekly therein. He sought to be a leader, a maker of the first path. He was covertly self-centered in all of his non-attributed work, let it be remembered.

As to critics see his Addison, Vol. 4, p. 148 to 151, and 221 to 223. That he wore a mask during his entire labors, see, please, Vol. 2, p. 10 to 17.

HIS POSTHUMOUS POCKET LABORS 151

In this connection we show where, in his own words, Bacon proclaimed his intention to make the world his heir. In the already mentioned Parliamentary speech concerning his "New Atlantis" and his great revenue project, he, among other things, says:

"For by this unchargeable way, my lords, have I proposed to erect the academical fabric of this island's Solomon's House, modelled in my New Atlantis. And I can hope, my lords, that my midnight studies, to make our countries flourish and outvie European neighbors in mysterious and beneficent arts, have not so ungratefully effected your noble intellects, that you may delay or resist his Majesty's desires, and my humble petition in this benevolent, yea, magnificent affair; since your honorable posterities may be enriched thereby, and my ends are only to make the world my heir, and the learned fathers of my Solomon's House, the successive and sworn trustees in the dispensation of this great service, for God's glory, my prince's magnificence, this parliament's honor, our country's general good, and the propagation of my own memory." No vision, note its "sworn trustees," and later its aims p. 95 and 154.

He had earlier to Queen Elizabeth said in Sonnet 6 that she would make worms her heir, if she failed of issue.

It is indeed a sad thing that some of the most significant work Francis Bacon ever wrought should thus be kept out of sight. Were Dr. Rawley and others conversant with his cypher methods, members of this secret order, and "the good pens that forsake me not?" If there was ever a Baconian piece, this speech surely was one. We give it in full in our "Defoe Period" p. 18 to 21. See then p. 234 to 237, and 589. We say it concerns

Bacon's secret South Sea revenue scheme, tacked to his "New Atlantis" and thwarted by the sharpers as set out in earlier pages. Thinking this speech not Bacon's, Mr. Spedding fails to give it. Why, with his reasons did he not give it, and leave the reader to judge? See, please, why he fails to give it. "Bacon's Letters," Vol. 7, p. 199, 200. Then see p. 235.

Are not its words "the propagation of my own memory" in full accord with Sonnet 55 and with his last will made but four months prior to his supposed death, wherein his "cabinets," "boxes," and "presses," are said to contain "that durable part of my memory, which consisteth of my works and writings." Posterity Drama! How unless with the "cabinets," "boxes," and "presses," reader, was Bacon to make the world his heir?

In his Carlyle waif, the "Hero Worship," p. 388, he, touching books, and the "Hero as Man of Letters" says: "Certainly the art of writing is the most miraculous of all things man has devised. Odin's *Runes* were the first form of the work of a Hero; *Books*, written words, are still miraculous *Runes*, of the latest form. In Books lies the *soul* of the whole Past Time; the articulate audible voice of the Past, when the body and material substance of it has altogether vanished like a dream. Mighty fleets and armies, harbours and arsenals, vast cities, high-domed, many-engined,—they are precious, great: but what do they become? Agamemnon, the many Agamemnons, Pericleses, and their Greece; all is gone now to some ruined fragments, dumb, mournful wrecks and blocks; but the Books of Greece! There Greece, to every thinker, still very literally lives; can be called up again into life. No magic *Rune* is stranger than a Book. All that Mankind has done, thought, gained or been: it is lying as in magic preservation in the pages of Books. They are the chosen possession of men."

In them, in books, Bacon strove ever to reveal himself; to reveal his mental accumulations; his mental clothing for the good of men. Ease, in the detail of his Art, as shown in his Shakespeare; in his Crusoe; in his Gulliver; in his "Holy War;" in his "New Atlantis;" in his Milton; made it ever a delight to him. He says "But the images of men's wits and knowledges remain in books, exempted from the injuries of time and capable of perpetual renovation." As to their protection from the injuries of time, let the reader turn to Milton's prose works, Bohn's edition, Vol. 2, p. 48 to 102 and read attentively the article entitled "Areopagitica." We will maintain Bacon's authorship of it against all critics.

The article is structured against the restraint by law of the publication of books, which it claims first began with the inquisition of Rome, and on page 62 we have: "Till then books were ever as freely admitted into the world as any other birth; the issue of the brain was no more stifled than the issue of the womb; no envious Juno sat cross-legged over the nativity of any man's intellectual offspring." The "New Organ," be it remembered, was first outlined as a birth, the birth of time. Fear of restraint upon publication of the author's own works rests here.

The critics say the measured prose tread of Bacon shows he could not have been a great poet. Yet Milton, with the same prose tread; they crown as chief in that art.

As in Shakespeare we have Bacon's scope treatise on mind or metaphysics; so in Milton we have his scope treatise on theology. The two claimed absentees, or missing links, from Bacon's great system here present themselves.

From the Plays, the wilderness, the field of temptation, we may now advance through varying pabulum to Milton, to Moses' chair; and thence to the Temple, or Solomon's House.

Macaulay, of Bacon, says, "What he was as a natural philosopher and moral philosopher, that he was also as a theologian." Dr. Rawley, in his preface to Bacon's "New Atlantis" first published in 1627, the year following Bacon's supposed death, says: "This fable, my Lord devised, to the end that he might exhibit therein a model or description of a college instituted for the interpreting of nature and the producing of great and marvellous works for the benefit of men, under the name of Solomon's House, or the College of the Six Days Works." Let it now be called to direct relation with Milton's six days work of creation. From it, p. 146 we quote:

"Thus you see we maintain a trade, not for gold, silver, or jewels; nor for silks; nor for spices; nor any other commodity of matter; but only for God's first creature, which was *Light;* to have *light* (I say) of the growth of all parts of the world."

Again: "The End of our Foundation is the knowledge of Causes, and secret motions of things; and the enlarging of the bounds of Human Empire, to the effecting of all things possible." "Bacon's Phil. Works," Vol. 3, p. 156.

By the "New Atlantis," Bacon's "Formula of Interpretation," his "Time's best jewel" of Sonnet 65 was, we say, to be borne undisclosed to posterity. Its wonder resides in its scale of ascending and descending axioms found by means of his "Tables of Discovery" eternized in Sonnet 122. This as yet undisclosed "Formula" is the light itself of his "New Organ;" his new system of induction. The system can be opened only by means of it. This "Formula" is its only door. There is no climbing up or entrance to the system in any other way.

The system opens in an investigation into the origin or law of light, which Bacon says "is God's first creature." It begins with transparent bodies, as water, glass, crystal, etc. By change in the configuration of their particles, he at once moves to colors, as by whipping water or pounding glass, they thus become white; the union of all colors. He finds the secrets of nature to lie in configuration. He says: "Knowledge of the configuration of bodies is as new a thing as the discovery of forms." All color in bodies results from difference in configuration. "For all color is the broken image of light," says Bacon. This field, fully traced will show the wonders in nature which lie in colors. Objects to the mind, and our dealings with them, make up our existence. If all color be removed from an object, to human ken, remove we not the object? We here touch Bacon's subtle, his distinctive views concerning matter and substance. He speaks ever of the substance of the human soul; the substance of the divine. This subtlety may be traced in all of the works here called under review, Milton included. Manifestations to sense are ever products of motion, with Bacon's views; and this he applies to light as to all other parts of operating nature. Touching the origin itself, of light, Bacon says; "There has been no inquiry." Touching this; touching configuration; and touching "the freeing of a direction to find the form" or law of light; or any one of the "simple natures," see please our presentation at page 67 to 71.

This brings us to a definite point. Returning to transparent bodies, the reader may have noticed that we did not mention air. "Air" says Bacon "is a permanent body." It is not subject to the changes in nature of other transparent bodies. It is not compounded. It never forsakes its fluidity. It is the body through which all other bodies in nature are seen. And so from his Milton, using herein Everyman's Library edition, we, from page 103 touching air, quote thus:

"Air, and ye Elements, the eldest birth
Of Nature's womb, that in quaternion run
Perpetual circle, multiform, and mix
And nourish all things, let your ceaseless change
Vary to our great Maker still new praise."

See "O ancient Powers of Air," page 274. See then Bacon on air, "Phil. Works," Vol. 5, p. 460 to 500. And on p. 315 we have: "Therefore, whereas flame is a momentary and air a fixed substance, the living spirit partakes of the nature of both." Let air in this sense in the Plays be traced from "Areal," in "The Tempest," to that "most tender air" in act 5 scene 4 and 5 of "Cymbeline."

Trace air and fire in Sonnet 45, "the first my thought, the other my desire." We in this Sonnet have Bacon's strange word "recured," and explained in Milton p. 264. We find Bacon using such expressions as "the wombs of the elements," "the womb of nature," "the womb of

earth," "the womb of time," "the bosom of nature,"
"nature is God's art," "mind is the divine fire," "heat
and cold are nature's two hands," "the church is the
eye of England," "divinity is the art of arts," "the
human mind is the seat of providence," "God's stage,"
"God's theatre," "God's curtain," "God's placets,"
"the substance of the human soul," "the substance of
the divine" and the like.

Touching Bacon's use of this word "substance," see
our presentation at p. 75 and 155. And from the angel
Rapheal's speech to Adam in Milton p. 110 we have:

"O Adam, one Almighty is, from whom
All things proceed, and up to him return,
If not depraved from good, created all
Such to perfection; one first matter all,
Endued with various forms, various degrees
Of substance, and, in things that live, of life;
But more refined, more spirituous and pure,
As nearer to him placed or nearer tending
Each in their several active spheres assigned,
Till body up to spirit work, in bounds
Proportioned to each kind. So from the root
Springs lighter the green stalk, from thence the
   leaves
More aery, last the bright consummate flower
Spirits odorous breathes: flowers and their fruit,
Man's nourishment, by gradual scale sublimed,
To vital spirits aspire, to animal,
To intellectual; give both life and sense,
Fancy and understanding; whence the Soul
Reason receives, and Reason is her being,
Discursive, or Intuitive: Discourse

> Is oftest yours, the latter most is ours,
> Differing but in degree, of kind the same.
> Wonder not, then, what God for you saw good
> If I refuse not, but convert, as you,
> To proper substance."

This is a Bacon text reader, from which a volume might be written. The thoughts involved in it are all found in chapter 3, book 4 of Bacon's "De Augmentis." Touching the word "substance," we quote him thus: "The doctrine concerning the breath of life, as well as the doctrine concerning the substance of the rational soul, includes those inquiries touching its nature,—whether it be native or adventive, separable or inseparable, mortal or immortal, how far it is tied to the laws of matter, how far exempted from them; and the like." "Phil. Works," Vol. 4, p. 397. As to "divine substance" see Milton page 31, 37, 88, 130.

Touching the "To vital spirits aspire, to animal, to intellectual," see please, our "Defoe Period" p. 52 to 57, where we give full Baconian proofs in this.

Note now in Raphael's speech that "Reason" in the angels is "Intuitive," while in Adam it is "Discursive," that is, by way of "Discourse." So in Hamlet we have "A beast that wants discourse of reason would have mourned longer." As to the difference between human reason, and the sagacity of brutes, Bacon says: "Again, let the nature in question be "Discourse of Reason." "Phil. Works," Vol. 4, p. 179. So we have it in Bacon, in Milton, and in the plays.

"Discourse of Reason"! Where, reader, save in the writings under review, will be found this most distinctive expression?

Animal life, though conscious, is not self-conscious. That wonder, instinctive intelligence, though working through the animal, is still not of it. The formative vessels that structure and sustain its body, show even more wonder than that manifested in its outer life. The dog it is true may seek the lowest point to jump the fence. So when a bone is broken, the formative vessels will step outside their usual work and repair the breech. Self-conscious life starts at zero; and by culture, widens ever. Instinct improves not upon its methods. The animal is born with its gifts. The bird builds its first nest; the bee its first comb; as perfectly as they can ever build them. A kitten dropped into water, before ever its eyes have been opened to its surroundings, will swim; and as perfectly as it can ever swim. The babe, so dropped, drowns at once. It must stay for culture. The first breath of the chick bursts its prison walls, and within an hour it struts forth with its perfected gifts. Existence presents us with but three orders of intelligence; instinctive, ideational, creative. Creative intelligence structures and sustains objects to the mind. Ideational intelligence is self-conscious of, and deals with them, has "discourse of reason." Instinct here is broken up and functions into self-consciousness, into self-hood. The mere animal, though conscious, cannot differentiate its life from its environments. Until this line be broken, biology remains unsolved. Forces unseen back every manifestation to sense. You here have our own speech, reader, touching Instinct.

Again, on the previous page, in Milton, p. 109, we have:

"For know, whatever was created needs
To be sustained and fed. Of Elements

> The grosser feeds the purer; Earth the Sea;
> Earth and the Sea feed Air; the Air those Fires
> Ethereal, and, as lowest, first the Moon;
> Whence in her visage round those spots, unpurged
> Vapours not yet into her substance turned.
> Nor doth the Moon no nourishment exhale
> From her moist continent to higher Orbs.
> The Sun, that light imparts to all, receives
> From all his alimental recompense
> In humid exhalations, and at even
> Sups with the Ocean."

As to this feeding of the elements we from "Timon of Athens," Act 4, Scene 3 quote thus:

> "The sun's a thief, and with his great attraction
> Robs the vast sea: the moon's an arrant thief,
> And her pale fire she snatches from the sun:
> The sea's a thief, whose liquid surge resolves
> The moon into salt tears: the earth's a thief,
> That feeds and breeds by a composture stol'n
> From general excrement."

Note this word "excrement" as used in the plays, and in Bacon's attributed works. It will be found a good point in the proof of authorship. Note "excrementitious moisture." Sweat, nails, hair, and feathers, treated as excrements. In feathers study colors.

As to the words "Of Elements the grosser feeds the purer," we quote Bacon thus: "For in proportion as substances degenerate in purity and freedom of development, so do their motions degenerate. Now it happens, that as in point of velocity the higher planets move faster, and the lower less fast; so also the higher planets make spirals more closely coincident and coming nearer to circles, the lower make spirals more disjoined and further apart. For continually as they descend they recede more and more both from that height of velocity and that perfection of circular motion, in regular order." "Phil. Works," Vol. 5, p. 553, and see p. 539.

As to "those fires Ethereal, and as lowest, first the Moon," we in connection with Sonnet 107 have shown that Bacon regarded the moon as lowest down, and as the last sediment of earthly, and the first rudiment of heavenly, or self-sustained flame; and that at the height or body of the moon flame first begins to roll itself into globes, while at the sun, flame is on her throne. See p. 110.

Bacon's knowledge came rather from grounds or notions within himself, than from books, said Dr. Rawley. Touching the origin itself of light see Bacon's views in our presentation at page 74. And in his Milton, see please, p. 151. And on p. 153 we have:

"For, of celestial bodies, first the Sun
A mighty sphere he framed, unlightsome first,
Though of ethereal mould; then formed the Moon
Globose, and every magnitude of Stars,
And sowed with stars the heaven thick as a field.
Of light by far the greater part he took,
Transplanted form her cloudy shrine, and placed
In the Sun's orb, made porous to receive
And drink the liquid light, firm to retain
Her gathered beams, great palace now of Light.
Hither, as to their fountain, others stars
Repairing in their golden urns draw light,
And hence the morning planet gilds her horns;
By tincture or reflection they augment

Their small peculiar, though, from human sight
So far remote, with diminution seen.
First in his east the glorious lamp was seen,
Regent of day, and all the horizon round
Invested with bright rays, jocund to run
His longitude through heaven's high road; the grey
Dawn, and the Pleiades, before him danced,
Shedding sweet influence. Less bright the Moon
But opposite in levelled west, was set,
His mirror, with full face borrowing her light
From him; for other light she needed none
In that aspect, and still that distance keeps
Till night; then in the east her turn she shines,
Revolved on heaven's great axle, and her reign
With thousand lesser lights dividual holds,
With thousand thousand stars, that then appeared
Spangling the hemisphere."

We touch the word "jocund" in the foregoing, as Bacon uses it in the Plays, in the "Pilgrim's Progress," in the "Sartor Resartus" and throughout these writings. He says: "With arts voluptuary I couple arts jocular; for the deceiving of the senses is one of the pleasures of the senses." "Phil. Works," Vol. 4, p. 395. In his "Romeo and Juliet," he says:

"Night's candles are burnt out, and jocund day
  Stands tiptoe on the misty mountain tops."

In the "Pilgrim's Progress," "Now when Feeble-mind and Ready-to-halt saw that it was the head of Giant Despair indeed, they were very jocund and merry."

Touching now the earth itself we from Milton, p. 151 have:

"The Earth was formed, but, in the womb as yet
Of waters, embryon immature, involved,
Appeared not; over all the face of Earth
Main ocean flowed, not idle, but, with warm
Prolific humour softening all her globe,
Fermented the great mother to conceive,
Satiate with genial moisture; when God said,
'Be gathered now, ye waters under heaven,
Into one place, and let dry land appear'!"

Note here the earth, as mother of the system. In his view of the heavens, or on celestial motions, Bacon differed from all writers either of his own, or of the present day. Those under review, being his, are in accord. Contrary to the established, or Copernican system, Bacon believed that the earth and not the sun, was its center; and that the heavens revolved about it, as a center. He says: "For let no one hope to decide the question whether it is the earth or heaven that really revolves in the diurnal motion, until he has first comprehended the nature of spontaneous rotation." "Phil. Works," Vol. 4, p. 123. His "Theory of the Heavens" should now be read in full. See "Phil. Works," Vol. 5, p. 547 to 560. From its opening paragraph we have:

"I will myself therefore construct a Theory of the Universe, according to the measure of the history as yet known to us; keeping my judgment however in all points free, for the time when history, and by means of history my inductive philosophy, shall have been further advanced. Wherein I will first propound some things respecting the matter of the heavenly bodies, whereby their motion and construction may be better understood; and then I will bring forward my thoughts and views concerning the motion itself, which is now the principal question. It seems then that nature has in the distribution of matter separated fine bodies from gross; and assigned the globe of the earth to the gross, and the whole space from the surface of the earth and waters to the very extremities of the heaven, to the fine or pneumatic, as the two primary classes of things, in proportions not equal indeed, but suitable."

A little further on he says: "The pneumatic bodies which are found here with us (I speak of such as exist simple and perfect, not compound and imperfectly mixed), are those two, "Air and Flame." See, please, Sonnet 45. Note "naked," not compounded.

A sentence or two further on we have, "Now for these two great families of things, the Airy and the Flamy; we have to inquire upon what conditions they have taken possession of by far the greatest part of the universe, and what office they have in the system. In the air next the earth, flame only lives for a moment, and at once perishes. But when the air begins to be cleared of the exhalations of the earth and well rarefied, the nature of flame makes divers trials and experiments to attain consistency therein, and sometimes acquires a certain duration, not by succession as with us, but in identity; as happens for a time in some of the lower comets, which are of a kind of middle nature between successive and consistent flame; it does not however become fixed or constant, till we come to the body of the Moon. There flame ceases to be extinguishable, and in some way or other supports itself." We return to bodies "such as exist simple," not compounded. These concern "the simple natures." Bacon says: "For all compounds (to one that considers them rightly) are masked and clothed; and there is nothing properly naked except the primary particles of things." From his Essay on "Cupid; or, an Atom." See "naked," "Defoe Period" p. 42, please. Note that Bacon used word "Compound," here, in the plays, and throughout. In Sonnet 71 we have "When I perhaps compounded am with clay." See also Sonnet 118 and 125.

Touching now the earth as stationary, we, page 551, have "The earth then being stationary (for that I now think the truer opinion), it is manifest that the heaven revolves in a diurnal motion, the measure whereof is the space of twenty-four hours or thereabouts, the direction from east to west, the axis of revolution certain points (which they call poles) north and south." A sentence or two earlier he says: "I shall not stand upon that piece of mathematical elegance, the reduction of motions to perfect circles, either eccentric or concentric, or that high speech, that the earth in comparison to heaven is a point and not a quantity, or many other fictitious inventions of astronomers; but remit them to calculations and tables." Also see, "Phil. Works," Vol. 4, p. 348 to 373.

We now permit Francis Bacon to place the above points on "celestial motions" into the mouth of our first parent, Adam. This he does in his Milton, "Paradise Lost." Book 8, p. 161 where we have:

"When I behold this goodly frame, this World,
Of Heaven and Earth consisting, and compute
Their magnitudes—this Earth, a spot, a grain,

>   An atom, with the Firmament compared
>   And all her numbered stars, that seem to roll
>   Spaces incomprehensible (for such
>   Their distance argues, and their swift return
>   Diurnal) merely to officiate light
>   Round this opacous Earth, this punctual spot,
>   One day and night, in all their vast survey
>   Useless besides—reasoning, I oft admire
>   How Nature, wise and frugal, could commit
>   Such disproportions, with superfluous hand
>   So many nobler bodies to create,
>   Greater so manifold, to this one use,
>   For aught appears, and on their Orbs impose
>   Such restless revolution day by day
>   Repeated, while the sedentary Earth
>   That better might with far less compass move,
>   Served by more noble than herself, attains
>   Her end without least motion, and receives,
>   As tribute, such a sumless journey brought
>   Of incorporeal speed, her warmth and light:
>   Speed, to describe whose swiftness number fails."

Raphael replies to Adam, page 162, thus:

>   "To ask or search I blame thee not; for Heaven
>   Is as the Book of God before thee set,
>   Wherein to read his wondrous works, and learn
>   His seasons, hours, or days, or months, or years
>   This to attain, whether Heaven move or Earth
>   Imports not, if thou reckon right; the rest
>   From Man or Angel the great Architect
>   Did wisely to conceal, and not divulge
>   His secrets, to be scanned by them who ought

Rather admire. Or, if they list to try
Conjecture, he his fabric of the Heavens
Hath left to their disputes—perhaps to move
His laughter at their quaint opinions wide
Hereafter, when they come to model heaven,
And calculate the stars; how they will wield
The mighty frame; how build, unbuild, contrive
To save appearances; how gird the Sphere
With Centric and Eccentric scribbled o'er,
Cycle and Epicycle, Orb in Orb.
Already by thy reasoning this I guess,
Who art to lead thy offspring, and supposest
That bodies bright and greater should not serve
The less not bright, nor Heaven such journeys run;
Earth sitting still, when she alone receives
The benefit. Consider, first, that great
Or bright infers not excellence. The Earth,
Though, in comparison of Heaven, so small,
Nor glistering, may of solid good contain
More plenty than the Sun that barren shines,
Whose virtue on itself works no effect,
But in the fruitful Earth; there first received,
His beams, unactive else, their vigour find.
Yet not to Earth are those bright luminaries
Officious, but to thee, Earth's habitant.
And, for the Heaven's wide circuit, let it speak
The Maker's high magnificence, who built
So spacious, and his line stretched out so far,
That Man may know he dwells not in his own—
An edifice too large for him to fill,
Lodged in a small partition, and the rest
Ordained for uses to his Lord best known.

>   The swiftness of those Circles attribute,
>   Though numberless, to his omnipotence,
>   That to corporeal substances could add
>   Speed almost spiritual."

The genesis of his own great mission, Bacon places later in Adam's speech, p. 167 to 179. Did space permit we would gladly particularize the foregoing speech.

Many of the Psalms Bacon turned into verse. From the 104th, touching the mentioned unmoving or "sedentary earth," we quote him thus:

> "In the beginning, with a mighty hand,
>   He made the earth by counterpoise to stand;
>   Never to move, but to be fixed still;
>   Yet hath no pillars but his sacred will."
>   "Literary Works" by Spedding, Vol. 2, p. 281.

Touching now this "counterpoise," this pendant earth, we from Milton p. 98 quote thus:

> "Wherein all things created first he weighed,
>   The pendulous round Earth with balanced air
>   In counterpoise, now ponders all events,
>   Battles and realms."

As to this "pendulous round earth," and "this balanced air," in Milton, Bacon says: "And let not any unskillful person be astonished if it be made a question whether globes of compact matter can remain pendulous. For both the earth itself floats pendulous in the middle of the surrounding air, which is an exceedingly soft thing; and great masses of watery clouds and stores of hail hang in the regions of the air, whence they are rather forced down than fall of themselves, before they begin to feel the neighbourhood of the earth." "Phil. Works," Vol. 5, p. 537. See also Vol. 4, p. 425, where we have: "Inquire whether the quantity of a body can be so increased as entirely to lose the motion of gravity; as in the earth, which is pendulous, but falls not."

Points like these, we could quote until the reader was tired, did space permit. In his Milton, Bacon details briefly his knowledge touching both the scriptures and his distinctive philosophy of the heavens. He says "knowledge is the image of existence." We say, Milton is the image of his knowledge. In any event, reader, we here give you some bits of good literature.

What value has a critic's opinion, as to the authorship of this great work who has never spent an hour in the investigation of the subtle questions here under review?

The earth Bacon believed to be the mother of nature; and that all radiations into space came from, and would ultimately return to her; and that she was both nature's womb and tomb. And so in his "Romeo and Juliet," Act 2, Scene 3, we have:

"The earth, that's nature's mother, is her tomb;
What is her burying grave, that is her womb;
And from her womb children of divers kind
We sucking on her natural bosom find:
Many for many virtues excellent,
None but for some, and yet all different."

Touching now this "womb," and "tomb" or grave of nature, see Milton, page 51. And in his "Hamlet," Act. 2, Scene 2, Bacon says:

"This goodly frame, the earth, seems to me a sterile promontory; this most excellent canopy, the air, look you, this brave o'erhanging firmament, this majestical roof fretted with golden fire, why, it appeareth nothing to me but a foul and pestilent congregation of vapours."

None of nature's powers seemed more mysterious to Bacon than those of the winds. See please, our "Defoe Period," p. 40 to 52. They concern final causes and are handled alike by all of the Sages. Note the subterranean and other winds throughout. See p. 150, 213, 222, 232 and 319 in Milton.

The reader may of certainty, know Bacon's authorship of Milton if he will but famaliarize himself with Bacon's "Theory of the Heavens;" with his brief Histories of "Dense and Rare;" "History of the Winds;" "History of Life and Death;" "Description of the Intellectual Globe;" and his "Principles and Origins According to the Fables of Cupid and Coelum."

The last mentioned subject as to the two ancient "Fables," Bacon opens thus: "It is of the elder that I am now going to speak. They say then that this Love was the most ancient of all the gods, and therefore of all things else, except Chaos, which they hold to be coeval with him. He is without any parent of his own; but himself united with Chaos begat the gods and all things. By some however it is reported that he came of an egg that was laid by Nox." Again, "But his principal and peculiar power is exercised in uniting bodies; the keys likewise of the air, earth, and sea were entrusted to him." Again, "This Chaos then, which was contemporary with Cupid, signified the rude mass or congregation of matter." "Phil. Works," Vol. 5, p. 461. On page 468 he says: "For it is not written that God in the beginning created matter, but that he created the heaven and the earth." Creation then was the calling of the forces of Chaos into order, and thereafter their government. See Milton, p. 150.

Ever in Bacon's sense of use we now touch "Chaos," "Nox," "Hot, Cold, Moist and Dry," in Milton. See "Chaos," Milton, p. 9, 50 to 57. And on p. 50 we have:

"Before their eyes in sudden view appear
The secrets of the hoary Deep—a dark
Illimitable ocean, without bound,
Without dimension; where length, breadth, and highth,
And time, and place, are lost; where eldest Night
And Chaos, ancestors of Nature, hold
Eternal anarchy, amidst the noise
Of endless wars, and by confusion stand.
For Hot, Cold, Moist, and Dry, four champions fierce,
Strive here for mastery, and to battle bring
Their embryon atoms: they around the flag
Of each his faction, in their several clans,
Light-armed or heavy, sharp, smooth, swift, or slow,
Swarm populous, unnumbered as the sands
Of Barca or Cyrene's torrid soil,
Levied to side with warring winds, and poise
Their lighter wings. To whom these most adhere
He rules a moment: Chaos umpire sits,
And by decision more embroils the fray
By which he reigns: next him, high arbiter,
Chance governs all. Into this wild Abyss,
The womb of Nature, and perhaps her grave,
Of neither Sea, nor Shore, nor Air, nor Fire,
But all these in their pregnant causes mixed
Confusedly, and which thus must ever fight,
Unless the Almighty Maker them ordain
His dark materials to create more worlds."

Let now the mentioned "Hot, Cold, Moist and Dry," be carefully noted, as we shall later call them to proof relation with Bacon's "Capital Letter Cypher."

"Chaos," in Milton, represents a contending or warring period of the elements prior to creation; that is, prior to the six days work. Their contending grounds, is what Bacon calls "the middle region of the air." The good, the unembodied guardian spirits of this region, we touch later in Chapter 5. As to the warring of the mentioned elements of "Hot, Cold, Moist and Dry," see "Bacon's Letters," Vol. 1, p. 124; and "Phil. Works," Vol. 5, p. 479, 480, 532 and 533. Note "moist and dry" on page 489. As to dense and rare, we on page 477 have:

"That density and rarity are but the textures and, as it were, the webs of heat and cold, heat and cold being the producers and operatives thereof; cold condensing and thickening the work, heat separating and extending it."

Bacon as already stated, says: "Heat and cold are Nature's two hands." Note the emphasis upon these two words throughout Milton. Note these two tables in his "New Organ."

Returning to the "four champions fierce," "Hot, Cold, Moist and Dry" we quote Bacon thus: "I shall speak presently upon the question, *whether the stars are real fire;* and more fully and accurately in my precepts concerning the history of Virtues, where I shall treat of the origins and cradles of Heat and Cold, a subject hitherto unknown and untouched by men." "Phil. Works," Vol. 5, p. 533. Then see p. 509.

The mentioned "History of Virtues" is a reference direct to what constitutes Bacon's great "Alphabet of

Nature." He of it says, "This is a history reserved to myself." "Phil. Works," Vol. 5, p. 135; see p. 208, 426, 509 and 510. See also "Phil. Works," Vol. 4, p. 29 and 262. It concerns the already mentioned forms or laws of "the simple natures." They constitute the "Alphabet" and will be touched later. Let the student of English literature pause here for reflection.

As to the mentioned contending grounds; or Bacon's "middle region of the air," we from Milton p. 288 quote thus:

"For Satan, with sly preface to return,
Had left him vacant, and with speed was gone
Up to the middle region of thick air,
Where all his Potentates in council sat.
There, without sign of boast, or sign of joy,
Solicitous and blank, he thus began:—
Princes, Heaven's ancient Sons, Ethereal Thrones—
Demonian Spirits now, from the element
Each of his reign allotted, rightlier called,
Powers of Fire, Air, Water and Earth beneath.
(So may we hold our place and these mild seats
Without new trouble!)"

Touching now the mentioned "Powers of Fire, Air, Water and Earth beneath," Bacon says: "There is needed a history of the *Common Masses of Matter*, which I call the *Greater Colleges* (commonly called the *Elements*); for I find there are no accounts of fire, air, earth and water, with their natures, motions, operations, and impressions, such as to form a just body of history." "Phil. Works," Vol. 4, p. 299.

If the reader has not found Bacon in Milton, it is simply because he has failed to investigate a subtle subject.

Having touched briefly Bacon's astronomy and philosophy, in Milton, we turn next to mythology, the cradle in which Francis Bacon rocked his "new born child," his philosophy, from the beginning. It was rocked, however, in its restored or Hebrew, instead of in the Greek cradle, reader.

Bacon believed the Greek fables, in other words the Greek mythology, to be of Hebrew origin, but corrupted by the Greeks. To restore what he thought their true interpretation was the business of his "Wisdom of the Ancients." As an example, see first his restored interpretation of the fable "Cupid; or an Atom"; then of the fable "Pan." We from it quote thus:

"The ancients have given under the person of Pan an elaborate description of universal nature. His parentage they leave in doubt. Some call him the son of Mercury; others assign him an origin altogether different; saying that he was the offspring of a promiscuous intercourse between Penelope and all her suitors. But in this the name of Penelope has doubtless been foisted by some later author into the original fable. For it is no uncommon thing to find the more ancient narrations transferred to persons and names of later dates; sometimes absurdly and stupidly, as in this instance; for Pan was one of the oldest gods, and long before the times of Ulysses; and Penelope was for her matronly chastity held in veneration by antiquity."

Touching the fable itself he says: "A noble fable this, if there be any such; and big almost to bursting with the secrets and mysteries of Nature.

Pan, as the very word declares, represents the universal frame of things, or Nature. About his origin there are and can be but two opinions: for Nature is either the offspring of Mercury—that is of the Divine Word (an opinion which the Scriptures establish beyond question, and which was entertained by all the more divine philosophers): or else of the seeds of things mixed and confused together. For they who derive all things from a single principle, either take that principle to be God, or if they hold it to be a material principle, assert it to be though actually one yet potentially many; so that all difference of opinion on this point is reducible to one or other of these two heads,—the world is sprung either from Mercury, or from all the suitors. He sang, says Virgil,

> How through the void of space the seeds of things
> Came first together; seeds of the sea, land, air,
> And the clear fire; how from these elements
> All embryos grew, and the great world itself
> Swelled by degrees and gathered in its globe.

The third account of the generation of Pan, might make one think that the Greeks had heard something, whether through the Egyptians or otherwise, concerning the Hebrew mysteries; for it applies to the state of the world, not at its very birth, but as it was after the fall of Adam, subject to death and corruption. For that state was the offspring of God and Sin,—and so remains. So that all three stories of the birth of Pan (if they be understood with a proper distinction as to facts and times) may be accepted as indeed true. For true it is that this Pan, whom we behold and contemplate and worship only too much, is sprung from the Divine Word, through the medium of confused matter (which is itself God's creature), and with the help of sin and corruption entering in.

To the Nature of things, the Fates or destinies of things are truly represented as sisters. For natural causes are the chain which draws after it the births and durations and deaths of all things, their fallings and risings, their labours and felicities:—in short all the fates that can befall them." Bacon's "Literary Works" by Spedding, Vol. 1, p. 707 and 709.

Bacon here presents an example of his interpretation, weeding, and reverence for, these fables. It should be read in full. That he did not believe them of Greek origin, clearly appears from his introduction to the work. From it, page 697, we have: "But the consideration which has most weight with me is this, that few of these fables were invented, as I take it, by those who recited and made them famous,—Homer, Hesiod, and the rest." See now our "Defoe Period," p. 518 to 521.

These fables served as a kind of framework upon which to hang his literary doings. They concern his "places of invention." In the foregoing quotation note his strange words as to the fall of Adam," for that state was the offspring of God and Sin,—and so remains." This he explains in his Milton p. 61, 46 to 55 and 234. See p. 212, 221 to 227 and 264 to 267. On p. 265 it is said "Sin and Death" are Satan's "two main arms." Did Bacon believe that sin is, and was designed to be, the carver of human life? See Sonnet 119.

Touching now "the ways to death," see Milton, p. 244 to 249. In Bacon's "History of Life and Death," note this distinctive expression "the ways to death," also "the porches of death." Bacon's "Phil. Works," Vol. 5, p. 222, 311, 315, or, our "Defoe Period," p. 58 and 60.

In the introduction to Bacon's crowning work his "Novum Organum," he, as to the fable Scylla, says: "So that the state of learning as it now is, appears to be represented to the life in the old fable of Scylla, who had the head and face of a virgin, but her womb was hung round with barking monsters, from which she could not be delivered. For in like manner the sciences to which we are accustomed have certain general positions which are specious and flattering; but as soon as they come to particulars, which are as the parts of generation, when they should produce fruit and works, then arise contentions and barking disputations, which are the end of the matter and all the issue they can yield." "Phil. Works," Vol. 4, p. 14. Bacon made these fables forms upon which to hang ideas. He thus made ideas quick, vivid and retentive. In his interpretation of this fable, in his "Wisdom of the Ancients," he says it furnishes "reflections without end." In his technical sense of use he touches it in his Milton p. 44 thus:

"Before the gates there sat
On either side a formidable Shape.
The one seemed woman to the waist, and fair,
But ended foul in many a scaly fold,
Voluminous and vast—a serpent armed
With mortal sting. About her middle round
A cry of Hell-hounds never-ceasing barked
With wide Cerberean mouths full loud, and rung
A hideous peal; yet, when they list, would creep,
If aught disturbed their noise, into her womb,
And kennel there; yet there still barked and howled
Within unseen." See p. 48.

The most ancient of these fables seem to have impressed Bacon with extreme reverence and as if they concerned fixed laws of being. And so in, Book 7 of "Paradise Lost," p. 145 we have:

> "Descend from Heaven, Urania, by that name
> If rightly thou art called, whose voice divine
> Following, above the Olympian hill I soar,
> Above the flight of Pegasean wing!
> The meaning, not the name, I call; for thou
> Nor of the Muses nine, nor on the top
> Of old Olympus dwell'st; but, heavenly-born,
> Before the hills appeared or fountain flowed,
> Thou with Eternal Wisdom didst converse,
> Wisdom thy sister, and with her didst play
> In presence of the Almighty Father, pleased
> With thy celestial song. Up led by thee,
> Into the Heaven of Heavens I have presumed,
> An earthly guest, and drawn empyreal air,
> Thy tempering. With like safety guided down,
> Return me to my native element;
> Lest, from this flying steed unreined (as once
> Bellerophon, though from a lower clime)
> Dismounted, on the Aleian field I fall,
> Erroneous there to wander and forlorn.
> Half yet remains unsung, but narrower bound
> Within the visible Diurnal Sphere.
> Standing on Earth, not rapt above the pole,
> More safe I sing with mortal voice, unchanged
> To hoarse or mute, though fallen on evil days,
> On evil days though fallen, and evil tongues,
> In darkness, and with dangers compassed round,
> And solitude; yet not alone, while thou

Visit'st my slumbers nightly, or when Morn
Purples the East. Still govern thou my song,
Urania, and fit audience find, though few.
But drive far off the barbarous dissonance
Of Bacchus and his revellers, the race
Of that wild rout that tore the Thracian bard
In Rhodope, where woods and rocks had ears
To rapture, till the savage clamour drowned
Both harp and voice, nor could the Muse defend
Her son. So fail not thou who thee implores;
For thou art heavenly, she an empty dream."

Touching now Bacon's views of Hesperian fables or "gardens of the Muses," see please, Milton, p. 80; our "Defoe Period," p. 197. In his "Essay on Gardens," he says: "God Almighty first planted a garden. And indeed it is the purest of human pleasures." In his "Natural History," note his wonderful knowledge of flowers, trees and gardens. Note here the second period, or story but half told.

To show, in addition to our earlier quotation from him that Bacon regarded the Greek fables not of Greek, but of Hebrew origin, we, from his Milton, p. 317 quote thus:

"All our Law and Story strewed
With hymns, our Psalms with artful terms inscribed,
Our Hebrew songs and harps, in Babylon
That pleased so well our victor's ear, declare
That rather Greece from us these arts derived—
Ill imitated while they loudest sing
The vices of their deities, and their own,
In fable, hymn, or song, so personating
Their gods ridiculous, and themselves past shame.
Remove their swelling epithets, thick-laid

> As varnish on a harlot's cheek, the rest,
> Thin-sown with aught of profit or delight,
> Will far be found unworthy to compare
> With Sion's songs, to all true tastes excelling,
> Where God is praised aright and godlike men,
> The Holiest of Holies and his Saints
> (Such are from God inspired, not such from thee);
> Unless where moral virtue is expressed
> By light of Nature, not in all quite lost.
> Their Orators thou then extoll'st as those
> The top of eloquence—statists indeed,
> And lovers of their country, as may seem;
> But herein to our Prophets far beneath,
> As men divinely taught, and better teaching
> The solid rules of civil government,
> In their majestic, unaffected style,
> Than all the oratory of Greece and Rome.
> In them is plainest taught, and easiest learnt,
> What makes a nation happy, and keeps it so,
> What ruins kingdoms, and lays cities flat;
> These only, with our Law, best form a king."

This government with its great senate, its single legislative body, is described in Milton p. 260. See it set forth now in his prose works, Vol. 2, p. 108 to 138 for the government of England following the execution of the King, Charles the 1st.

From the foregoing it may be clearly seen, touching mythology or these fables, "That rather Greece from us these arts derived." In other words, from the Hebrews, rather than the Greeks, these fables took their origin. This surely was the opinion of the author of Milton, whoever he may have been.

Returning now to "Urania" in the first of these quotations, let it be noted that it is that which she personates, that is intended to be addressed. Murray in his "Mythology," p. 140 says: "The proper home of Themis was Olympus, and hence she was styled Urania." He continues: "She was a personification of divine will as it bore upon the affairs of the world, and accordingly the Delphic oracle had been under her control before it was yielded to Apollo, to whom, as her successor, she communicated the prophetic art." She was the Muse of astronomy, see p. 179.

It may thus be observed, she was of an earlier origin than Apollo. He becomes now the leader of the nine Muses, and on p. 177 Murray says:

"In addition to the usual nine we hear of three other Muses—Melete, Mneme, and Aoede, who are described as daughters of Uranus, and supposed to have existed from the earliest times. As, however, both Homer and Hesiod appear to know only the number nine, we may assume that the belief in the existence of the other three must have originated in the speculations of comparatively later times."

In the Carlyle, "Hero Worship," p. 263 we have: "Who knows to what unnameable subtleties of spiritual law all these Pagan Fables owe their shape! The number *Twelve* divisiblest of all, which could be halved, quartered, parted into three, into six, the most remarkable number,—this was enough to determine the *Signs of the Zodiac*." Let it be remembered there were twelve tribes of the Children of Israel.

Note "empyreal air" in our late quotation from Milton." This is a direct reference to the "Empyrean." See p. 57, 147, 157, 160, 214 and 215.

As to "empyrean," we from Bacon quote thus:

"Between the globe of the earth then and the summits of heaven there seem to be generally three regions especially remarkable; namely, the tract of the air, the tract of the planetary heaven, and the tract of the starry heaven. Now in the lowest of these tracts, the starry nature is not consistent; in the middle it is consistent, but gathers into separate globes; in the highest it diffuses itself among a great number of globes, till at the summits thereof it seems to pass as it were into the perfect empyrean." See "Phil. Works," Vol. 5, p. 521 to 524.

"Pegasean wing," the symbol of poetic inspiration, used in our "Urania" quotation, refers, we say, to "The Horse I ride," in the "Sartor Resartus" to be touched later. See the wonders of this horse described in Murray, p. 52, 54, 84, 186 and 219.

As to the words "yet not alone, while thou visit'st my slumbers nightly" see please, Sonnet 86 touching "that affable familiar ghost which nightly gulls him with intelligence." Then see "Milton", p. 10, 56, 146 and 178. See then the Defoe work, "Duncan Campbell," and Addison, Vol. 2, p. 10 to 17, remembering we are here but outlining. It is said Bacon dictated his night thoughts every morning to his secretary. See please, as to sleep, dreams and visions, our "Defoe Period," p. 259 to 270.

As to the mentioned fable of "Bacchus" or Dionysus, see its interpretation in Bacon's "Wisdom of the Ancients" as well as the fable of "Cupid, or an Atom". The most ancient Cupid has been touched in connection with Chaos. He bears direct relation to Bacon's doctrine of forms of the first class; and so concerns metaphysics.

The later Cupid, the son of Venus, has relation to physics; and so to his forms of the second class. They will be touched in due place. Bacon said be it remembered, "poetry is the stream of knowledge." Dionysus here, note, was not the Areopagite.

As to the "Thracian bard" or Orpheus, see its interpretation in Bacon's "Wisdom of the Ancients." Note the application or kind of use he made of it; and generally of these fables. "Bacon's Letters," Vol. 4, p. 117.

What, in his interpretation of the fable "Pan," did Francis Bacon mean by the "Hebrew Mysteries?" See please, what he says in our "Defoe Period," p. 75 as to the doctrine concerning "the sacred ceremonies." He says "it discloses and lays bare the very mysteries of the sciences." This he says in connection with cypher writings, and methods for handing writings on to posterity. The business of fables is to teach ideas, not facts. Bacon ever so used them. They concern allegory. They symbolize thought. Note later in his "Sartor Resartus" its Chapter on Symbols, to be called to relation with his "Symbol Cypher," so called. Touching this method of instruction by fables, this web of entertainment, we from his "Grubean Sage" Defoe, quote thus:

"The humour of the day must prevail; and as there is no instructing you, without pleasing you, and no pleasing you but in your own way, we must go on in that way; the understanding must be refined by allegory and enigma; you must see the sun through the cloud, and relish light by the help of darkness; the taste must be refined by salts, the appetite whetted by bitters; in a word, the manners must be reformed in masquerade, devotion quickened by the stage, not the pulpit, and wit be brightened by satires upon sense." "Defoe Period," p. 68, Addison, same subject, p. 70.

Careful thought will yet reach the conclusion, that the "Pilgrim's Progress," in Baconian light, concerns the government of the individual; the "Holy War" the government of a people—England; Milton the government of the world, or God's government of the twelve tribes. His volume on mind or metaphysics, is the Plays; so Milton is his great volume to posterity, on his distinctive views in astronomy, philosophy and theology.

God's special government as king, to the time of Saul; of the twelve tribes of Israel, is symbolized, by the twelve stones in the breast-plate of Aaron, and a stone besides. So in like manner, was Bacon's "New Atlantis." See its twelve heads, and one concealed please, in our "Defoe Period," p. 381 to 384.

As to these twelve stones, "and a stone besides," we from Milton, p. 69, quote thus:

"The place he found beyond expression bright,
Compared with aught on Earth, metal or stone—
Not all parts like, but all alike informed
With radiant light, as glowing iron with fire.
If metal, part seemed gold, part silver clear;
If stone, carbuncle most or chrysolite,
Ruby or topaz, to the twelve that shone
In Aaron's breast-plate, and a stone besides,
Imagined rather oft than elsewhere seen—
That stone, or like to that, which here below
Philosophers in vain so long have sought;
In vain, though by their powerful art they bind
Volatile Hermes, and call up unbound
In various shapes old Proteus from the sea,
Drained through a limbec to his native form."

Note here, and on p. 151 "like with like," to be touched later.

From Bacon's "Wisdom of the Ancients" let "Proteus" be called to relation. Among other things Bacon says: "He was the messenger and interpreter of all antiquity and all secrets." He says: "The sense of this fable relates, it would seem, to the secrets of nature and the conditions of matter. For under the person of Proteus,—Matter—the most ancient of all things, next to God—is meant to be represented."

In "The Two Gentlemen of Verona," Proteus is made one of its chief characters. As to God's special government itself, both civil, and ecclesiastic, of the twelve tribes, we from Milton, p. 260 quote thus:

"This also shall they gain by their delay
In the wide wilderness; there they shall found
Their government, and their great Senate choose
Through the twelve tribes, to rule by laws ordained.
God, from the Mount of Sinai, whose grey top
Shall tremble, he descending, will himself,
In thunder, lightning, and loud trumpet's sound,
Ordain them laws—part, such as appertain
To civil justice; part, religious rites
Of sacrifice, informing them, by types
And shadows, of that destined Seed to bruise
The Serpent, by what means he shall achieve
Mankind's deliverence. But the voice of God
To mortal ear is dreadful: they beseech
That Moses might report to them his will,
And terror cease; he grants what they besought,
Instructed that to God is no access
Without Mediator, whose high office now

>Moses in figure bears, to introduce
>One greater, of whose day he shall foretell,
>And all the Prophets, in their age, the times
>Of great Messiah shall sing.   Thus laws and rites
>Established, such delight hath God in men
>Obedient to his will that he vouchsafes
>Among them to set up his tabernacle—
>The Holy One with mortal men to dwell,
>By his prescript a sanctuary is framed
>Of cedar, overlaid with gold; therein
>An ark, and in the ark his testimony,
>The records of his covenant; over these
>A mercy-seat of gold, between the wings
>Of two bright Cherubim; before him burn
>Seven lamps, as in a zodiac representing
>The heavenly fires."

Here again we touch the shadows, types, or teaching by the "sacred ceremonies," in other words the Hebrew mysteries. Bacon of his "initiative" method of transmitting of writings to posterity says: "I call that doctrine initiative (borrowing the term from the sacred ceremonies) which discloses and lays bare the very mysteries of the sciences." See our p. 175; then "Defoe Period," p. 75 and p. 70 to 77.

God's special government, of the twelve tribes by law given direct through Moses and the High Priests continued until the destruction of the first Temple. The Gospel, or new mode of teaching, that is, the new dispensation by the Son, followed. See Milton, p. 62, 262 to 270. Bacon's government model, found elsewhere in these writings will be touched later. In the prose writings of Milton the model was retailored and the doctrine of the divine right of kings sharply cut out.

That the renewed earth may be our ultimate or restored Paradise, see Milton p. 266, 268, 63 and 65. The terrene, instead of the solar system, is maintained in Milton as in Bacon throughout. Hence the emphasis in Milton upon the earth's value in the system. In other words the earth, and not the sun, is its center, contrary to modern thought.

As to the stupendous bridge over Chaos from Hellgate to the earth, see please Milton, p. 212 to 232. As to freedom of the will, divine substance, the deadly sins, their arguments, and this bridge, see p. 29 to 59. The tagging, hooking, or buttoning together of Bacon's divine works to form a bridge, will be touched latter in Chapter 5 in connection with his "Capital Letter Cypher." He not only says, "nature is God's art," but that "divinity is the art of arts."

With this brief outlining, we would now; using our replete vowel indexes upon these writings, gladly enter upon an extended examination of the vocabulary, distinctive expressions, and language features in Milton, in all their Baconian relations, as taken into said indexes did space permit. In a measure they may be found in the foot-notes to our "Defoe Period." Note on p. 188, 222 and 455 Bacon's tentative methods with words. Let others spin upon the thread here drawn out.

Throughout Bacon's attributed writings almost nothing appears in relation to himself. More will be found, in his non-attributed works. The sum almost of what he says of himself, in his attributed writings, will be found in the already mentioned paper touching the handing on of his writings to posterity quoted at page 111. It concerns his Life aims and believed in mission. Having earlier taken shape in his mind, let it be read here in connection with his words in Milton, p. 278, with which we close this chapter:

> "When I was yet a child, no childish play
> To me was pleasing; all my mind was set
> Serious to learn and know, and thence to do,
> What might be public good; myself I thought
> Born to that end, born to promote all truth,
> All righteous things. Therefore, above my years,
> The Law of God I read, and found it sweet;
> Made it my whole delight, and in it grew
> To such perfection that, ere yet my age
> Had measured twice six years, at our great Feast
> I went into the Temple, there to hear
> The teachers of our Law, and to propose
> What might improve my knowledge or their own,
> And was admired by all. Yet this not all
> To which my spirit aspired. Victorious deeds
> Flamed in my heart, heroic acts—one while
> To rescue Israel from the Roman yoke;
> Then to subdue and quell, o'er all the earth,
> Brute violence and proud tyrannic power,
> Till truth were freed, and equity restored:
> Yet held it more humane, more heavenly, first
> By winning words to conquer willing hearts,
> And make persuasion do the work of fear
> At least to try, and teach the erring soul,
> Not wilfully misdoing, but unware
> Misled; the stubborn only to subdue."

In calling the foregoing to relation with the quotation referred to, note its words, "myself I thought born to that end, born to promote all truth." Note "truth" in Sonnet 101.

At the opening of Milton, p. 10, and see p. 56, 146, 178, we have

> "Fast by the oracle of God, I thence
> Invoke thy aid to my adventrous song,
> That with no middle flight intends to soar
> Above the Aonian mount, while it pursues
> Things unattempted yet in prose or rhyme.
> And chiefly thou, O Spirit, that does prefer
> Before all temples the upright heart and pure,
> Instruct me, for thou know'st; thou from the first
> Wast present, and, with mighty wings outspread,
> Dove-like sat'st brooding on the vast Abyss,
> And mad'st it pregnant: what in me is dark
> Illumine, what is low raise and support;
> That, to the highth of this great argument,
> I may assert Eternal Providence,
> And justify the ways of God to men."

If Francis Bacon be judged by that which he has done for the race, under his great covert mission, would he be entitled to be called St. Alban, reader?

CHAPTER V.

THE FIELD OF INVENTION. RELATION OF THE SCIENCES TO POETRY. CYPHERS OF BOTH LITERARY PERIODS. THE UNDISCLOSED OVERALL CYPHER OF THE SECOND. THIS THE TRUE KEY. THE "SARTOR RESARTUS" BACON'S WORK OF DURANCE. CONTAINS IT THE "ALPHABET"?

FRANCIS BACON began early, and was ever, an astute student of the ancients. In his survey of the state of learning he reports a history of literature wanting. To supply that history was part of his great covert mission. His expressed purpose "to hunt the utmost antiquity and mysteries of the poets," rests here. He says: "For poetry is, as it were, the stream of knowledge." It presents the field of Invention, and is aided by all of the sciences. This is graphically portrayed in the Plays, and throughout the writings under review. In a non-attributed work he says:

"Poetry I regard as a tender virgin, young and exceedingly beautiful, whom diverse other virgins,—namely, all the other sciences—are assiduous to enrich, to polish and adorn. She is to be served by them, and they are to be ennobled through her. But this same virgin is not to be rudely handled, nor dragged through the streets, nor exposed in the market place, nor posted on the corners of gates or palaces. She is of so exquisite a nature that he who knows how to treat her will convert her into gold of the most inestimable value. He who possesses her should guard her with vigilance, neither suffering her to be polluted by obscene, nor degraded by dull and frivolous works."

CYPHER ARTS OF BOTH PERIODS 191

Bacon here, on the relation of the sciences to poetry, is elegantly and clearly portrayed. Let it be observed that poetry is included as one of the sciences. "Metaphysics, or final causes, are as a virgin consecrated to God," says Bacon.

The "virgin" here represents "final causes." She represents the region of Invention, which is aided by "all of the other sciences,"—and "they are to be ennobled through her." They are her true handmaids.

She presides over literature. She is "the stream of knowledge." She in his Shakespeare Sonnets, is his Muse. See Sonnet 100 and others. She is "that best I wish in thee," after his fall, see Sonnet 37. To the King he then said, "I am still a virgin, for matters that concern your person or crown." His Promus Note 380 is in these words: *"To me, O virgin! no aspect of sufferings arises new or unexpected; I have anticipated all things and gone over them beforehand in my mind."*

His distinctive metaphysics is presented in the first named virgin. With his views, she is the head, the apex, the virgin key to the sciences. She was the "blessed key" of Sonnet 52.

She is beautiful, in that it is the business of final causes to reveal phenomena. See our "Defoe Period," p. 194. "Including final causes with physics, has caused an arrest and prejudice to science," says Bacon.

In metaphysics Francis Bacon differs from all other writers. He says: "Be not troubled about Metaphysics, when true Physics have been discovered, there will be no Metaphysics. Beyond the true Physics is divinity only." Again, "It is the perfect law of the inquiry of truth, that nothing be in the globe of matter, which has not its parallel in the globe of crystal or the understanding."

Mind with his views is the cause of all; whether expressed by divine will in creation, or presented to human ideation, by objects. Ever, in a sense peculiarly his, he refers to mind or soul as a "substance," in the sense of cause, or law; as the substance of heat, is the law of heat; and akin to the thought, "For soul is form and doth the body make."

Let "substance," and "the great eye of the world" be traced in our "Defoe Period," p. 534 to 542. See then on "substance," his Addison, Vol. 4, p. 104; and the article beginning on p. 112. Then p. 1 to 5 see the matchless paper on the resident gifts of the human soul. "Sleep is nothing else but the retirement of the living spirit into itself," says Bacon. The body is its "outward walls," Sonnet 146. Dream life discloses its possibilities. See please our "Defoe Period," p. 258 to 271. Mind is a "castle," see Defoe "History of the Devil," Bohn's edition, p. 443, 568 and 576. When spread in the body it is in its outer walls, is in eye-gate, ear-gate, nose-gate, mouth-gate and feel-gate.

"Substance" in Bacon's distinctive sense of use is found in both Plays and Sonnets, and throughout these writings, Milton included. See Sonnet 53. His mental philosophy may be found epitomized in Sonnet 146.

Formal or final causes, only, with Bacon's views, concern mind or metaphysics; so material and efficient causes concern physics, clothing, or body. Note in this his Tabular system, and his subtle doctrine of Forms; as applied to metaphysics; in his own sense of use.

Francis Bacon's Posthumous Pocket labors; his great literary scheme for posterity, began in early years;

and, being assisted by methods not yet known to us, grew to great proportions.

Into relation with this thought; we, from that Pocket, introduce here a Waif, that time will yet distinguish. Like his Shakespeare Sonnets, it is in a sense autobiographic. It might properly yea should be printed under the same cover.

Its "Paper—catacombs," will yet tell of Francis Bacon's infancy, his youth, his romance, his wanderings in the wilderness of doubt and unbelief, his new flooring of knowledge; and, in its "New Mythus;" his ultimate religious convictions; which, to this hour, remain mooted questions. From it, we of the Poet and Instructor, quote thus:

"What too, are all Poets, and moral Teachers, but a species of Metaphorical Tailors? Touching which high Guild the greatest living Guild-brother has triumphantly asked us: "Nay, if thou wilt have it, who but the Poet first made Gods for men; brought them down to us; and raised us up to them?" Note "Tailor," our p. 76.

This great "Guild-brother" we say reader was Francis Bacon himself; and as surely as he was the man in hue; "all hues in his controlling," of the Shakespeare Sonnets 20 and 53, where "in Grecian tires" he tells us he is "painted new."

In his "Wisdom of the Ancients," he restored Greek fables, to their Hebrew roots. Thus used; he, in them, was "painted new," as stated in the Sonnet.

Were portions of these restored fables made to stand for his already named "simple natures;" or "surds?" He at one time thought to bring forth his new system under cover of them, as Mr. Spedding informs us. See our p. 49.

In most of Bacon's non-attributed work, we find him adroitly, yet covertly, self-centered. In what Francis Bacon did for the race, he started at home, started in his own soul and studied its emotions, its motives, its passions, as well as its objective activities; and with it, and with all the impetus which he could gather to it, from both research and imagination did he paint forth every phase of our human life. With his views one age is but a type of all ages; and one soul but a type of the souls of all. For these reasons we find him largely, though covertly self-centered in his work. He was the radius from which to insinuate all knowledge. He was indeed the Great Monk, that retired not his thoughts nor his body, but who hooded his personality from portions of his works; leaving them thus to time.

As stated he avoids self-laudation, as did Dante, Horace and Homer; by addressing himself in cover words—pronouns in the second and third person, instead of the first. This applies in general throughout his non-attributed work when he refers to himself; though not in every instance. We illustrate our point by a brief example from Swift:

"Thou shalt in puny wood be shown,
Thy image shall preserve thy fame;
Ages to come thy worth shall own,
Point to thy limbs, and tell thy name."

"Men are made of wood," says Bacon. And "I am no unlikely piece of wood to make your Lordship a good servant." His servant "Sages" were his "Classic Authors in Wood," reader; and he their lauded chief.

"This, O Universe! is the adventurous attempt of me thy secretary."

The author of our "Guild-brother" work, known as the "Sartor Resartus," himself pronounces it to be, the greatest piece of work he has, or ever hopes to perform. See Bohn's edition, p. 335. In our quotation from it, note, please the use of entirely uncalled for capital letters. They are spread thus throughout the entire work. We would now place it.

We believe it to be the most concentrated piece of linguistic Art known to our language. Touching language, and to further emphasize its strange use of capitals, we p. 90 quote thus:

"Language is called the Garment of Thought, however, it should rather be, Language is the Flesh-Garment, the Body of Thought. I said that Imagination wove this Flesh-Garment; and does she not? Metaphors are her stuff; examine Language; what, if you except some few primitive elements (of natural sound), what is it all but Metaphors, recognized as such, or no longer recognized; still fluid and florid, or now solid-grown and colorless. If those same primitive elements are the osseous fixtures in the Flesh-Garment, Language,—then are Metaphors its muscles and tissues and living integuments." See here Bacon's very distinctive views on fantasy; or on the Imagination and Reason; and notably in connection with "similitudes, types, parables, visions, dreams." "Defoe Period," p. 193 to 195, 269 and 586.

We say to you, reader, this work consists in tagging, hooking, or buttoning together, into one body of Art; the entire framework, or salient points in both of Francis Bacon's literary periods. The Second period followed his fall, in 1621; and was, in a measure, the retailoring and expanding of the First. Already we have touched it to relation in connection with his Shakespeare Sonnet 68, in Chapter IV, p. 105. This Sonnet must ever indicate the line of demarkation between Francis Bacon's First, and Second, literary periods.

We now call our "Guild-brother" work to direct relation with Francis Bacon's "Capital Letter Cypher," in other words, to his great "Alphabet of Nature." Thus far it has been thought that this "Alphabet" was never completed or in any way put to use.

That the reader may here appreciate the value which Bacon himself set upon it, we give its closing words thus:

"Such then is the rule and plan of the alphabet. May God the Maker, the Preserver, the Renewer of the Universe, of his love and compassion to man, protect and guide this work, both in its ascent to His glory, and in its descent to the good of man, through His only Son, God with us." "Bacon's Phil. Works," by Spedding, Vol. 5, p. 211 and 135.

As a legitimate inference of Bacon's authorship we quote the title to a Defoe work now kept out of sight. "An Essay upon Literature; or, an Enquiry into the Antiquity and Original of Letters; Proving, That the two Tables written by the Finger of God in Mount Sinai, was the first Writing in the World; and that all other Alphabets derive from the Hebrew." See in this our "Defoe Period," p. 429 to 432. Fine business surely for the liveryman Defoe. Remember please, the uncalled for use of capital letters in the mentioned papers attributed to him. Turn here, ye careful thinker, to his "History of the Devil," Bohn's edition, p. 294 to 300, and 332 to 342 if you would have light upon Defoe's; Milton's; that is, upon Bacon's authorship. He ever retailored and was his own critic.

The spring-head now set against the development of this authorship lies deep. But few are aware of its extent or subtlety. Let it be looked to that later it controls not the publication of Books. Its eye rests here. It has existed from the hour of the overthrow, in England, of the Cromwell party, the Independents. We touched it earlier at p. 144.

Why now Bacon's sacred emphasis, reader, upon his "Alphabet," if never completed or put to use? We say the most exquisite example of its use will yet be found in the "Sartor Resartus;" and we would that the world take note of it; and see to it; that works thus capitalized be carefully preserved from oblivion to the day of its true opening.

We understand Bacon himself to refer to it, the "Sartor Resartus;" in the Cypher story found in his "Novum Organum" by Mrs. Gallup, in her wonderful Work entitled "Francis Bacon's Bi-literal Cypher," p. 123, where we have:

"Therefore there is soone to bee a little work which shall set cleerlie forth these artes that have held many, many a secret from my times to carry it on (to) th' great future. If there bee none to decipher it at length, how many weary days will have beene lost; yet—such is the constancy of hope in our brests—we hold to th' work without rest, firmly trusti'g that coming times and th' future men of our owne, and other lands, shall at last rewarde these labours as they soe manifestly shall deserve."

We say the Time Example in placing the "Alphabet," the Overall Cypher, will yet be found upon the

Title-page of The Great First Folio of his Shakespeare Plays, issued in 1623, where we have:

> "This Figure, that thou here seest put,
> It was for gentle Shakespeare cut;
> Wherein the Graver had a strife
> With Nature, to outdo the life.
> O, could he but have drawn his wit
> As well in brass, as he hath hit
> His face! the Print would then surpass
> All that was ever writ in brass.
> But, since he cannot, Reader, look
> Not on his Picture, but his Book."

Let the uncalled for use of capital letters in the foregoing, as in our "Guild-brother" work under review, be carefully noted. We were the first to lay the claim, that all of the poems introductory to the Shakespeare plays, were products of Francis Bacon's own pen, though other names are appended to them. See our "Defoe Period," p. 114.

Mrs. Gallup in her great Cypher Work not only finds, but sets out a short Cypher-story in every poem; and in every part of the introductory matter to the Plays; except in the mentioned title-page poem. See her work, p. 165 to 168.

She finds no Cypher story in the Time or title-page poem, we say, simply because it concerns the author's Second literary period; and so, she herself has not yet found it; or if so, she has not as yet made it public.

Thus far we say she has disclosed but the Cyphers and work of the First period; which, by design, and to save confusion, was intended to be first opened; before

CYPHER ARTS OF BOTH PERIODS 199

the Second period was to be entered upon; as we purpose now to make clearly manifest from Mrs. Gallup's own work. Careful examination of it, makes clear our already laid claim touching the Defoe period.

Bacon's endeavor to compass the Cypher work of both Periods; and yet hold the "Alphabet" in abeyance; or, for a time, undiscovered, by his decipherer; rendered the work difficult.

Now to our purpose. In the poem following the Title-page of the Plays, to wit;—in the Ben Jonson poem, Mrs. Gallup, p. 165, finds enwrapped the following:

"Any person using here the bi-literall Cipher, will find a rule to be followed when writing the hidden letters in which are Histories, Comedies, Tragedies; a Pastorall of the Christ; Homer's epics and that of Virgil, which are fully render'd in English poetry; the completion of my New Atlantis; Greene's Life; Story of Marlowe; the two secret epistles (expressly teaching a Cipher now for the first time submitted, doubtfully, for examination and studie, by any who may be sufficiently curious, patient, or industrious); part of Thyrsis (Virgile's Aeclogues); Bacchantes, a Fantasie; Queene Elizabeth's Life (as never before truely publisht); a Life of the Earl of Essex, and my owne.
Fr. Lord Verulam."

We now claim to the reader, that "the two secret epistles," and the words enclosed in parentheses, in the foregoing, refer to the, as yet, undisclosed "Alphabet of Nature," or Key to Bacon's new invention. Special use of parentheses was made in the cypher work. See our quotation, and see p. 143. Note "the two secret epistles" here; and p. 155, 136, 143, 146, 167 and 346.

To show the "Alphabet" to be as the goal of the work, we, from the Cypher found in the "Headings of the Comedies," p. 166, quote thus:

"Reade easy lessons first, and forsooth the Absey in the Life and Death of King John, act one, is a good one; it shewes the entrance to a labyrinth. Court Time, a sure leader, and proceed to his Alphabet of Nature."

Later we will return to the mentioned parenthesis, and to the Cypher in it; "now for the first time submitted," and show it to be the one which the author was unwilling his decipherer should at the outset discover.

Bacon's critics must erelong unhitch from their train of conclusions which say, he began a system he was unable to complete. The mentioned Key or "Formula" they never saw. In youth he outlined it as "The Noblest Birth of Time." This from the outset was the true wonder of the system; and it was never revealed by Bacon while living, is our claim. We are here and now in search of it, reader.

As to his felt mission, and mental gifts, we from Mrs. Gallup's Cypher Work, p. 344 quote him thus: "We that know the manifold mightie influences of unseen things, owe more of this knowledge of our environings to the light from our Celestiall Source then to our investigations. Therein lieth the duty we owe to our fellowe-men." See our p. 62 and 63.

As to the different Cyphers made use of by Bacon, see Mrs. Gallup, p. 167. And on page 118, he says: "These are the Bi-literall; Wordd; Capital Letter; Time, or as more oft call'd Clocke; Symboll; and Anagrammaticke."

CYPHER ARTS OF BOTH PERIODS   201

To show now that Francis Bacon did not intend to have his decipherer at once find the Key to his new invention, we in the Cypher Work found by Mrs. Gallup in his "New Organ," p. 127, quote thus:

"Therefore, whilst I am still in very good hope that my last contrivance is not solv'd, noe feeling of anie sort, save kindlinesse, is in my soule towards my decypherer.

If he discov'r the key of my newe invention, himselfe, before it bee explain'd, it shall redound to his credit."

"My last contrivance" was, we say, to teach "the key of my new invention." This "contrivance" reader, was the Cypher "now for the first time submitted." See please the parenthesis, found in our Cypher quotation from the Ben Jonson poem, p. 199. See "contrivance," our p. 87.

We say it was "Time's best jewel" of Sonnet 65; and, as yet, was not in "Time's chest" therein mentioned. Note, please, this "chest" in Sonnet 48, where he refers to his jewels—his literary works.

It was the "blessed key" that could bring the author to his "sweet uplocked treasure" of Sonnet 52.

We say, this Key was revealed to Bacon through or by means of his "Tables of Discovery" referred to in Sonnet 122, and the absolutely new system of Sonnet 59.

These tables were the very ground, and root so to speak, upon which Francis Bacon reared his great philosophic structure for posterity. It was these that first revealed the forms of "the simple natures" as an Alphabet to it; and hence their laudation in the Sonnet.

The Shakesperean having for nearly three centuries failed to open these Sonnets, he should not longer pout.

That he may not longer blow out the light, we say: "No leave take I for I will ride as far as land will let me by your side." We have in our "Defoe Period" but traced a thread line. This erelong will become a highway to Sir Francis Bacon's English Augustan Age. "A history of literature is wanting," says Bacon.

The "pen-names" of his First literary period, became the "Grubean Sages" of the Second. As to pen-names, see the Cypher Work, p. 54 and 148. We on p. 54 have: "When I have assum'd men's names, th' next step is to create for each a stile naturall to th' man that yet should [let] my owne bee seene, as a thrid o' warpe in my entire fabricke soe that it may be all mine."

How Robert Harley came by the manuscripts of the Second period must yet be told. Did he play them for the author's or for his own ends? Our subject being new, we have indulged in some repetition.

The mentioned Sages stood about him, as in a theatre; or as the poets of the Roman Period did about Caesar. They spread Baconian light. They were Bacon's "multiplying glass." They were facets upon one and the same stone. They will yet be found to be radiations of intelligence from the one source; the one center; the one vocabulary; and that Bacon's. In Sonnet 76 we have: "Every word doth almost tell my name," so distinctive is his vocabulary. See our "Defoe Period" foot-notes, as to vocabulary and language features.

All of the "Newly Discovered Defoe Papers" present throughout the same identical use of capital letters as found in our "Guild-brother" work. They are what in journalism became known as leading articles. They were started after the close of the "Review" in 1713, it having begun in 1704. They all concern Cypher writing. Please see, in this, our "Defoe Period," p. 447 to 520. To this time, the first English daily; the first English magazine; and the first English novel; had not, as yet, appeared; and both literature and morals were at a low ebb, as Knight in his History of England informs us. See here the Britannica article on "Newspapers" to this period.

When literary works highly wrought are poured rapidly into a depleted period; it, of necessity, brings confusion of tongues. The design was, the destruction of the old, by growing beneath it a better new, in both church, and state. Bacon himself said he would set the ants anew at work; and a new awakening will yet come out of this literature, reader. Such a vast system of reform was never before attempted by any one man. And Bacon well knew it. Read Sonnet 55, with pronouns in the first person.

We now present an example of Bacon's pen-names in the person of Thomas Hobbes. He was a friend to both Bacon, and Ben Jonson, and became one of Bacon's "pen-names." His "Leviathan" was Bacon's government model of the First period. It has the same use of capital letters throughout. See the beautiful Cambridge University Press edition of the work.

Bacon's greatest concentration touching government, of both church and state, is here set out. Its first paragraph opens, in a description, of the model. This model is God's noblest form, nature's apex—the human body. "The King the head, we the body," says Bacon. The "Grubean Sages" all; were masters in portraying it. See our "Defoe Period," please, p. 573 and 595.

Touching this model we from the Cypher found in Bacon's Natural History by Mrs. Gallup, p. 359, quote thus:

"The times were not a bad schoolemaster. When I resumed my former study of th' state of th' nations, and patiently work'd out th' modell of government, my most potent reason may be justlie gather'd. In my Cipher as you must soon see, I have written out the aforesaid modell, which I still thinke is worthy of attention."

And on page 344 we have: "Surely my hand and braine have but short rest. I firmly beleeve it were not in the power of humane beings to do anie more than I have done, yet I am but partlie satisfied." Let the government model so elegantly portrayed in Coriolanus Act 1, sc. 1, especially the portion of it embracing the Belly and the Limbs, here entertain the reader.

In the "Leviathan" osseous or structural features of Bacon's work are with great concentration portrayed. Its identity in thought is spread into every phase of his First literary period. Its views on demonology, apparitions, dreams and visions, set out in its later Chapters, and spread into all the writings under review; are basic in character. They are here weeded to the scripture basis. In Chapter 47 we have covert knowledge expressed touching the Pope or King Oberon and his fairies. This knowledge is spread in many of the Plays. Note in this Chapter the already mentioned views con-concerning the Presbyterians and Independents. See our p. 133. As to Presbyterians Bacon says:

"Besides, they opened the people a way to government by their consistory and presbytery; a thing though in consequence no less prejudicial to the liberties of private men than to the sovereignty of princes, yet in the first show very popular." "Bacon's Letters," vol. 1, p. 100, see p. 96. See in this our "Defoe Period," p. 198 and 199, 215 and 228.

Note in the "Leviathan," Bacon's views, that to the time of Saul, God, in person, governed the world, as King since which time Kings became his deputies on earth. Everywhere in the Plays, the King is "God's deputy," "God's lieutenant;" "God's anointed;" "God's minister." And so in Richard 2nd, Act. 1, Sc. 2 we have:

"Lan. God's is the quarrel; for God's substitute,
His deputy anointed in His sight,
Hath caus'd his death; the which, if wrongfully,
Let Heaven revenge; for I may never lift,
An angry arm against His minister."

Soon after his fall as already indicated in the Sonnets, Bacon began vigorously to retailor this doctrine set out so fully in his "Leviathan." Later, he most effectually performed it in his Defoe's "Jure Divino" and other works. See our "Defoe Period," p. 545 and 568. On p. 515 and 516 he most graphically portrays his own folly in abandoning his defence. Join this please, reader, with "Thou blind fool, Love," of Sonnet 137 in our Chapter 4, p. 102.

We return here to the use of capital letters. Let the Addison article on the subject, Bohn's edition, Vol. 3, p. 102 to 105 be read in full. It closes in these words:

"This instance will, I hope, convince my readers, that there may be a great deal of fine writing in the capital letters which bring up the rear of my paper, and give them some satisfaction in that particular. But as for the full explication of these matters, I must refer them to time, which discovers all things." See now "parenthesis" Addison vol. 4, p. 107 to 110. On p. 108 we have: "I have read over the whole sentence, (says I) but I look upon the parenthesis in the belly of it to be the most dangerous part, and as full of insinuations as it can hold."

From that robe of durance the "Sartor Resartus" we page 121 quote thus: as to capital letters: "These things were the Alphabet, whereby in aftertime he was to syllable and partly read the grand Volume of the World: what matters it whether such Alphabet be in large gilt letters or in small ungilt ones, so you have an eye to read it?" And on p. 116, "I was looking at the fair illuminated Letters and had an eye for their gilding." See then p. 46, 90, 135, 227 to 299.

Think you reader, the only motive for the use of the uncalled for capital letters spread forth in the mentioned works, was but to disfigure the printed page? On the contrary, we now make manifest to the reader Bacon's distinctive use of them. In the Cypher found in his "New Organ" page 119, by Mrs. Gallup, he says:

"Keyes are used to pointe out the portions to be used in this worke. These keies are words imploied in a naturall and common waye, but are mark'd by capitalls, the parenthese, or by frequent and unnecessarie iteration; yet all these are given in the other Cypheres also making the decipher's part lesse difficile." A little further on: "These must bee noted specially since they form our series of combining or joyning wordes, which like the marks th' builder putteth on the prepar'd blockes of stone shewing the place of each in the finisht building, pointe out with unmistakable distinctness its relation to all other parts." We would quote further did space permit. Let now the points touching capital letters, and parentheses, be taken with us as we go. They are again referred to at p. 143.

In the same cypher p. 122, we have:

"It is not easie to reveal secrets at th' same time that a wall to guard them is built, but this hath beene attempted, how successfull it shal be, I know not, for tho'wel contrived, so no one has found it, the cleere assurance cometh onely in th' dreemes and visions of of th' night, of a time when the secret shall bee fully reveal'd. That it shall not be now, and that it shall be then—that it shall be kept from all eyes in my owne time to bee seene at some future daye, however distante— is my care, my studie."

We may thus see as already claimed, that Francis Bacon did not intend, while living, to have his Key, his "Formula of Interpretation" made public.

In the Cypher found in his "Natural History," p. 353, we understand him to make reference to this "Formula" in the words: "But no part is better worth noting than the portio' that doth containe the story which Time onely will reveale, inasmuch as it is nowhere found or is nowhere left to my countrymen but in Cypher."

Does our work of durance, the "Sartor Resartus," our "Guild-brother" work, contain that Cypher? We believe it, reader, and that Mrs. Gallup will erelong find it. We would assist. It is for the interest of literature that her Work be placed in our many good libraries.

Bacon's Posthumous labors, the Cypher story tells us, began at an early age.

Occurs it never to the readers of English literature that the Defoe period involves a mystery? While publishing the brief paper found in our "Defoe Period"

p. 30, the good Editor remarked, "I know not what you may have found, but to me, the Defoe period was ever a mystery." See our p. 125 and 144.

It was a literary stream, proceeding from anonymous writers having but the one Spring-head. The knowledge of each, to the fringes thereof, was known to, and interlocked with that of the others. This stream became the literary "English ink-sea" of the" Sartor Resartus," p. 282 and 275 to 282. The "sculptured stone head" of the "Fountain" from which it flowed, p. 23, is made manifest in Vol. 4, p. 172 to 175, and 218 to 221 of Addison. At times Addison is Swift; then Swift, Addison.

Returning to our government model in both church and state we from the "Sartor Resartus," page 45, quote thus:

"For neither in tailoring nor in legislating does man proceed by mere Accident, but the hand is ever guided on by mysterious operations of the mind. In all his Modes and habilatory endeavours an Architectural Idea will be found lurking; his Body and the Cloth are the site and materials whereon and whereby his beautiful edifice, of a Person, is to be built." And on p. 250, "For if Government is, so to speak, the outward SKIN of the Body Politic, holding the whole together and protecting it; and all your Craft-Guilds, and Associations for Industry, of hand or of head, are the Fleshly Clothes, the muscular and osseous Tissues (lying *under* such SKIN), whereby Society stands and works; then is Religion the inmost Pericardial and Nervous Tissue, which ministers Life and warm Circulation to the whole. Without which Pericardial Tissue the Bones and Muscles (of Industry) were inert, or animated only by a Galvanic vitality; the

CYPHER ARTS OF BOTH PERIODS 209

SKIN would become a shrivelled pelt, or fast-rotting raw-hide; and Society itself a dead carcass,—deserving to be buried." See here please, p. 312.

In the foregoing, Bacon again touches his "Leviathan" model. Note "muscular and osseous Tissues" of society, there used. Then note them as applied to language in our earlier quotation from the work, or from the work itself, touching "Language" p. 90. This strange use of uncalled for capital letters, so far as we are aware, has awakened no comment.

Society, in the work, is presented as founded upon cloth, p. 4, 45, 67, 91, 188, 201, 294 and 313. In the "Pilgrim's Progress" touching cloth we quote thus: "Then they took them, and had them to Mount Charity, where they showed them a man that had a bundle of cloth lying before him, out of which he cut coats and garments for the poor that stood about him; yet his bundle, or roll of cloth, was never the less." The Tailor in the "Tale of a Tale," p. 55 and 69, is presented as an idol, postured as a Persian emperor. Note his Art. Bacon's philosophy of government, as it touches Persia and the Persian Magic, should be here read. "Bacon's Letters," Vol. 3, p. 90 to 99. Mr. Spedding p. 89 says: "Whence Bacon derived his idea of the nature of the Persian Magic, is a question with which we need not trouble ourselves here." Bacon p. 90, says: "For there is a great affinity and consent between the rules of nature, and the true ruler of policy: the one being nothing else but an order in the government of the world, and the other an order in the government of an estate. And, therefore the education and erudition of the kings of Persia was in a science which was termed by a name then of great reverence, but now degenerate and taken in ill part: for the Persian magic, which was the secret literature of their kings, was an observation of the contemplations of nature and an application thereof to a sense politic; taking the fundamental laws of nature, with the branches and passages of them, as an original and first model, whence to take and describe a copy and imitation for government." And p. 92: "This knowledge then, of making the government of the world a mirror for the government of a state, being a wisdom almost lost (whereof the reason I take to be because of the difficulty for one man to embrace both philosophies) I have thought good to make some proof (as far as my weakness and the straits of time will suffer) to revive in the handling of one particular, wherewith now I most humbly present your Majesty." We here have both his obverse and reverse, or light and dark side in handling this subject. In his Letters, Vol. 1, p. 125, he says: "Therefore, no doubt the sovereignty of man lieth hid in knowledge; wherein many things are reserved which kings with their treasure cannot buy, nor with their force command; their spials and intelligencers can give no news of them, their seamen and discoverers cannot sail where they grow."

Persian Magic! Basic in its weedings of government both in church and state is his Defoe "History of Magic." The Magi it was, that had to do with ancient fables, and with God's special government of the 12 tribes. In his Hobbes' "Leviathan," in his Milton, his kinds of knowledge reveal themselves. In the work on Magic may be traced the sources from which Bacon collated his distinctive views on government, on astronomy, on substance, on spirits; and notably on those never embodied and never to be embodied; to wit, the guardian spirits, which occupy, not the planets but with Bacon's views "the middle regions" of the air; the contending grounds; touched earlier in Milton, p. 171 to 174. These spirits he touches to relation in the Defoe work on "Apparitions." See Talboys' edition. We are here tracing for you English literature, Reader. As to Milton, "I fly out of my feathers." In his "History of the Devil," "I took it up by another handle."

Note now in the "Sartor Resartus," p. 55, "the Persian Blacksmith" and Queen Elizabeth; and 109 the little piece of "Persian silk" that covered the baby face of Teufelsdrockh in the Basket, when first viewed by his foster parents—Sir Nicholas and Anne Bacon, we say—and the basket bearer his father Leicester. Note the "Fox" and the "Leicester shoe-shop," p. 244, "and the farewell service of his awl!" p. 245. See "Fox" in the Cypher work, p. 346, where we have: "And I shall rest ill in my minde for this manie a long day, least this fox may chance to be unkennelled too early." See p. 169, 348 and 350.

Turning now to the "Sartor Resartus" p. 82 we have:
"The beginning of all Wisdom is to look fixedly on Clothes, or even with armed eyesight, till they become *transparent*." It is the business of mind, ever to deal with objects, and so be clothed.

Touching now the tagging, hooking or buttoning together of the author's literary works, in the "Sartor Resartus;" as well as touching Pegasus; and his own body, see p. 278; and on p. 71, we have:

"It was in some such mood, when wearied and fore-done with these high speculations, that I first came upon the question of Clothes. Strange enough, it strikes me, is this same fact of there being Tailors and

Tailored. The Horse I ride has his own whole fell: strip him of the girths and flaps and extraneous tags I have fastened round him, and the noble creature is his own sempster and weaver and spinner, nay, his own bootmaker, jeweller, and man-milliner, he bounds free through the valleys, with a perennial rainproof court-suit on his body; wherein warmth and easiness of fit have reached perfection; nay, the graces also have been considered, and frills and fringes, with gay variety of colour, featly appended, and ever in the right place, are not wanting. While I—good Heaven!—have thatched myself over with the dead fleeces of sheep, the bark of vegetables, the entrails of worms, the hides of oxen or seals, the felt of furred beasts; and walk abroad a moving Rag-screen, overheaped with shreds and tatters raked from the Charnel-house of Nature, where they would have rotted, to rot on me more slowly! Day after day, I must thatch myself anew; day after day, this despicable thatch must lose some film of its thickness; some film of it, frayed away by tear and wear, must be brushed off into the Ashpit, into the Laystall; till by degrees the whole has been brushed thither, and I, the dust-making, patent Rag-grinder, get new material to grind down. O subter-brutish! vile! most vile! For have not I too a compact all-enclosing Skin, whiter or dingier? Am I a botched mass of tailors' and cobblers' shreds, then; or a tightly-articulated, homogeneous little Figure, automatic, nay, alive?" Pegasus or "the Horse I ride" is the symbol of poetic inspiration. See our presentation at p. 182. The Chapter on "The Dandical Body" we think in a measure tampered with. Like the Sonnets, the Chapters of the work may have been written at different periods. As to method, the author p. 42 says, "each part overlaps, and indents, and indeed runs quite through the other."

Having touched "the Horse I ride" as it concerns poetry, we touch him now, see p. 260, as mounted by Elizabeth's rightful successor. We from the Cypher Work p. 142 quote thus: "For such a triviall, unworthie, unrighteous cause was my birthrighte lost, and nought save the strong will of Elizabeth turned men from conspiracie t' place me on th' throne. To winne backe their loyalty she assum'd most kingly aires, and, upon occasion harrangued the army, riding upon a richly caparison'd horse before the lines, and naming herself th' King. I for dear life dare not to urge my claim, but hope that Time shall ope th' waye unto my rightfull honors."

As to this tagging and buttoning together of the writer's works into one body of Art see p. 36, 66, 67, 271 and others. The work covers selected material from the entire English Augustan Age, reader. See p. 42, 43 and 45 to 59.

From p. 89 we have: "All visible things are Emblems; what thou seest is not there on its own account; strictly taken, is not there at all: Matter exists only spiritually, and to represent some Idea, and *body* it forth. Hence Clothes, as despicable as we think them, are so unspeakably significant." Again "Men are properly said to be clothed with Authority, clothed with Beauty, with Curses, and the like. Nay, if you consider it, what is Man himself, and his whole terrestrial Life, but an Emblem; a Clothing or visible Garment for that divine ME of his, cast hither, like a light-particle, down from Heaven? Thus is he said also to be clothed with a Body."

And on p. 90, "Whatsoever sensibly exist, whatsoever represents Spirit to Spirit is properly a Clothing, a suit of Raiment, put on for a season, and to be laid off. Thus in this one pregnant subject of CLOTHES, rightly understood, is included all that men have thought, dreamed, done, and been: the whole External Universe and what it holds is but Clothing; and the essence of all Science lies in the PHILOSOPHY OF CLOTHES."

And p. 70: "So that this so solid-seeming World, after all, were but an air-image, our Me the only reality; and Nature, with its thousandfold production and destruction, but the reflex of our own inward Force, the phantasy of our Dream."

And, on p. 82, the author says: "For Matter, were it never so despicable, is Spirit, the manifestation of Spirit: were it never so honourable, can it be more? The thing Visible, nay the thing Imagined, the thing in any way conceived as Visible, what is it but a Garment, a Clothing of the higher, celestial Invisible, unimaginable, formless, dark with excess of bright?" And see p. 241. In Milton we have the same subtle views as to Matter and Spirit, and "Mind is its own place," p. 15. See our presentation p. 157. We touch here the "New Mythus."

Reform is the basic purpose of this work both in Church and State. It is an attempt to thwart old or existing forms of society by growing beneath them better new. See in this p. 251 and its Chapter "The Phoenix;" then its Chapter on "Symbols." As to the Church itself; see please p. 251, 273, 292, 308, 312, 317. Its new form, to be drawn forth from out these writings, was to be the "New Mythus," reader. This reform was to be by pen-gun, not by bayonet. See p. 130 and 292. Bacon's ideational scope was never equalled in any age or country. More than probable, is it, that Mrs. Eddy drew from this work chiefly; though not quite catching the author's views as to matter and force. He says, it will be remembered, "For forms are but figments of the human mind unless you will call the laws of action by that name." Note "Thought-forms, Space and Time," on p. 302.

The so called "Clothes-Volume," of the work, concerns the author's great literary carcass itself. So its "Paper Bags," in covert terms, yield a tentative autobiography of its author; of his infancy, his youth, his romance, his wanderings in the wilderness of doubt and unbelief, and of his ultimate new flooring of knowledge for posterity. As to the author's birth, infancy, and foster parents, see p. 137 to 143.

As now to the "Clothes-Volume" itself see p. 95; then p. 9, 33, 42, 45, 72, 81, 121, 214, 235, 241, 243, 251, 252, 298, 299 and 314.

As to the "Paper Bags" see first p. 94 and 95; then 9, 81, 129, 134, 135, 150, 159, 165, 175, 179, 217 and 231.

The author's emphasis upon duty and obedience is spread into every phase of these writings; see, please, how they took their root in him, p. 122 and 123.

As to his romance and one only love, see its Chapter on "Romance." Then into relation with it call Bacon's Cypher Story by Mrs. Gallup, p. 12, 79, 118, 173, 175, 345 and 361.

From the foregoing the reader may have a quick gathering of important points upon this rich piece of subtlety; the "Sartor Resartus;" and this whether or not he accepts our views concerning it. How this waif drifted from Bacon's Posthumous Pocket labors to the hands of Thomas Carlyle, may perhaps be found in "Bacon's Letters," Vol. 1, p. 1 to 16; Vol. 2, p. 2 to 5; and "Phil. Works," Vol. 3, p. 3 to 10.

In the "Sartor Resartus" as in the "Cromwell Letters and Speeches" Editor and author are but one and the same person. The business of an Editor is here, as there, but part of the method of production, and introduction, of the book. There is here but the one writer. Touching this, we from the work itself, p. 13 have: "Who or what such Editor may be, must remain conjectural, and even insignificant; it is a voice publishing tidings of the Philosophy of Clothes; undoubtedly a Spirit addressing Spirits; whoso hath ears let him hear."

Prof. Hudson opens his introduction to Everyman's Library edition of the work, thus: "One of the most vital and pregnant books in our modern literature, "Sartor Resartus" is also, in structure and form, one of the most daringly original. It defies exact classification. It is not a philosophic treatise. It is not an autobiography. It is not a romance. Yet in a sense it is all these combined." A little further on he fully agrees with us in the point that it has but the one writer and that the rest, as to an Editor, is but method. As it is so here, so is it in the "Cromwell Letters and Speeches."

Francis Bacon was nowhere more adroit, or subtle, than in introductions to his non-attributed writings. See in this, his introduction to his Plays, and to his "Tale of a Tub."

This method in the "Sartor Resartus," permits Bacon, the real author, to select and present desired features, not only from his life work, the "Clothes-Volume;" but from "the river of his History," the "Paper Bags." Both "Volume," and "Bags," are said to be the work of Prof. Diogenes Teufelsdrockh; and to come from "deep-thinking Germany" to the hands of a nameless British Editor to be aired to the English people; see p. 5 to 9. As to Diogenes and his Tub, see, please, p. 245; and earlier the author's "Tale of a Tub." As to Diogenes and the "philosopher's weed," see our "Defoe Period," p. 101 to 104 and 224.

Were the letters in the never before used surname Teufelsdrockh to aid in opening the Overall cypher? At p. 109 of the "Sartor Resartus" it is queried as to whether the veil or piece of Persian Silk covering the baby face in the Basket, nothing can be inferred as to the true name. The Overall, or Capital Letter cypher in the Cypher Work, p. 143 is referred to thus: "But it is by othe' devices, as in cloth o' Persian silk, a patterne soon openeth out of the confusio'. Any aventurous worker can easilie trace it if he doth get th' true art."

This Cypher is found presented in Bacon's "History of Henry the Seventh," written subsequent to his fall, where he claims to be the son of Queen Elizabeth, the Bacons being his foster parents. As the Queen refused to proclaim her covert marriage with her favorite, Leicester, this left Bacon with but an assumed name. Let this story as to the author's genesis as told in the Cypher Work, p. 137 to 144, be called to direct relation with it as told in the "Sartor Resartus," p. 103 to 113. Prof. T. calls himself a "Pilgrim," a "Wanderer," the "Son of Time," and in covert terms from the "Paper Bags" gives us an anatomy of his life pilgrimage and doings. See our p. 121; then 24.

Bacon's web of entertainment again presents itself. Here it is an acute stimulus to mental endeavor; and the work will not readily be forgotten. We trust the reader has not forgotten our claim touching his trip to Highgate and the Hague. When returned he to England? On p. 341; will "his archives one day be opened by Authority?" Note "Monmouth Street at the bottom of our own English ink-sea," p. 282.

Touching the author's pilgrimage and his "Pilgrim-staff;" see, please, p. 93, 178, 185, 217, 218 and 244. And on p. 251 note the Interpreter. Then note him in the "Pilgrim's Progress" and in the last paragraph of Bacon's "New Organ."

We return now, Reader, to "Hot, Cold, Moist and Dry," touched earlier from Milton, p. 171 to 174. Into relation with these four elements, we from the "Sartor Resartus," p. 96, quote thus:

"Over such a universal medley of high and low, of hot, cold, moist and dry, is he here struggling (by union of like with like, which is Method) to build a firm Bridge for British travellers. Never perhaps since our first Bridge-builders, Sin and Death built that stupendous Arch from Hell-gate to the Earth, did any Pontifex, or Pontiff, undertake such a task as the present Editor. For in this Arch too, leading, as we humbly presume, far otherwards than that grand primeval one, the materials are to be fished up from the weltering deep, and down from the simmering air, here one mass, there another, and cunningly cemented, while the elements boil beneath." Note this Bridge; and the value of a true Book p. 202. As to "chaining together," the books, that belong together to form the Bridge; see p. 242, 235, 236, and 303. As to this "Hell-gate" Bridge; see our page 187, and Milton p. 53. "It is fit to see how we can make a bridge from the present practice to the reformation"—says Bacon. In the light of the foregoing we now present the reader direct proof of Bacon's authorship; as well of Milton and the "Sartor Resartus;" as of his Cypher Work. They each interlock and prove the other. This will form a step on which our critic must fall down; or else oer-leap; for in his way it lies. Now to our purpose.

Note the above mentioned parenthesis; "(by union of like with like, which is Method);" and on p. 242 is said to be the author's only method. We now call to direct relation this parenthesis with Bacon's Cypher Work p. 345, where we have:

"My word-signs are scatt'red with most prodigall hand, not onely in the prose, but also in the diverse other workes. In many places you may finde them named as joyning-wordes, this manner shewing their use, which is to bring parts together. You must likewise keep in minde one very important rule: it is, that like must be joyn'd to like. Match each key with words of a like meaning, like nature, or like origin." And on p. 174 we have: "Studie Time's rule: kin is set by kin, like is joyn'd to like." And on p. 169: "Seeke the keyes untill all bee found. Turne Time into an ever present, faithfull companion, friend, guide, light, and way." Again on p. 94 we have: "The joining-words you see repeated so frequently, marke the portions which are to bee joyned together in th' perfect whole, even as in the modell.

It doth not rest with the stone-mason to shape or invent his planne,—this is prepar'd to his use,—so in this my temple, the model hath not fayl'd to limne as bold a designe, which th' decyphere' must dutifullie, and with patience, bring to perfection." See now this same question of "Like with Like" presented in Milton p. 69, 151 and 212. On p. 151 we have:

> "Throughout the fluid mass, but downward purged
> The black, tartareous, cold, infernal dregs,
> Adverse to life; then founded, then conglobed,
> Like things to like, the rest to several place
> Disparted, and between spun out the Air,
> And Earth, self-balanced, on her centre hung."

See now p. 171 our tracings of Bacon in Milton, as to "Hot, Cold, Moist and Dry."

And, so we see, the "Clothes-Volume" of the "Sartor Resartus" was being tagged, hooked and buttoned together by the different cypher Arts, reader. In earlier pages, p. 197, we have claimed the "Sartor Resartus" to include Bacon's greatest, or Overall cypher of his Second period, his "Alphabet of Nature," and which Mrs. Gallup has not, as yet, discovered. Nor p. 199 did Bacon wish to have it discovered by his decipherer until after the works of his First period had been evolved. See his own words in this, p. 201, as to this "last contrivance," the "key of my new invention."

So now from his Cypher Work, p. 129, he, to his decipherer says: "Many times I have a sense of my kinde companion's presence, yet at the bottom of every other desire, is a hope that this Cypher shall not have beene seene or read when my summons shall come. Therefore tranquillity is an impossible state, and I am torn betwixt feare that it bee too well hid, and a desire to see all my devices for transmitting this wondrous history, preserv'd and beque'th'd to a future generatio', undiscov'r'd."

This Cypher concerns; see our presentation at p. 199 and 201, "the two secret epistles (expressly teaching a Cypher now for the first time submitted, doubtfully, for examination, and study, by any who may be sufficiently curious, patient, or industrious)."

Touching the use of "parentheses" from the "Sartor Resartus," p. 38, we quote thus: "Of his sentences perhaps not more than nine-tenths stand straight on their legs; the remainder are in quite angular attitudes, buttressed up by props (of parentheses and dashes) and ever with this or the other tagrag hanging from them."

In the Cypher work itself, p. 167, the mentioned Cypher is said to be "my great Cypher of Cyphers." See also p. 127, 165, 218, 219, 353 and 356. And on p. 346 we have: "Seeke th' key-words if you would find th' secrets I shall write or anie alreadie told, for a newe name must now bee given him who shewes here written some pages of his hidden history. This you may finde clearly tolde in the Word-Cypher if it be still to seeke, but as I have mentioned it in severall places I must be allow'd the hope that you have found the letter I have written which contains the directions in itself for a Cypher of a very great valew for my purposes." See this letter and Cypher again referred to at p. 155. And on p. 349: "This Cypher then is of value to future generations." Then see please p. 353 as to this the Overall cypher of the Second period yet to be found, we say, in the "Sartor Resartus."

We have here in the mentioned Cypher a touch, not only of a new literary age, but of a new method of portraying it. The fact that the Cyphers in the works, written by Bacon after his fall, do not detail, either that event, or events thereafter; supports our claim. It is evidence, also, of the truth of Mrs. Gallup's great work. Now on p. 360 of it will be found material which we think definitely concerns the opening of this Second literary period.

To show from the author's own words that his "Sartor Resartus" covers a Second literary period, he, p. 230 says: "Writings of mine, not indeed known as mine (for what am I?), have fallen, perhaps not altogether void, into the mighty seedfield of Opinion; fruits of my unseen sowing gratifyingly meet me here and there. I thank the Heavens that I have now found my Calling; wherein, with or without perceptible result, I am minded diligently to persevere. 'Nay how knowest thou', cries he, but this and the other pregnant Device, now grown to be a world-renowned far-working Institution; like a grain of right mustard-seed once cast into the right soil, and now stretching out strong boughs to the four winds, for the birds of the air to lodge in,—may have been properly my doing? Some one's doing it without doubt was; from some Idea, in some single Head, it did first of all take beginning; why not from some Idea in mine?" Note "Second Youth," p. 214.

As, to "my works," see p. 194, 195, and 202, 216. And on p. 217 he says: "If I have had a second-crop, and now see the perennial greensward, and sit under umbrageous cedars, which defy all Drought (and Doubt); herein too, be the Heavens praised, I am not without examples; and even examplers." And contrasting his labors with those of Alexander he on p. 202 says: "Thou too art a Conqueror and Victor; but of the true sort, namely over the Devil: thou too hast built what will outlast all marble and metal, and be a wonder-bringing

City of the Mind, a Temple and Seminary and Prophetic Mount, whereto all kindreds of the Earth will pilgrim." Touching the "Architect" and "Hodman" see p. 130.

Touching now this "Temple," and Alexander, see, please, our p. 107 to 109; then p. 140.

In the Cypher Work, of this temple, p. 171 Bacon says: "When the partes are separated, put all matter of like kinde together in boxes, which have been so marked with keies and joining-wordes that you may follow the plans with ease, not carefull for the outcome, since I am Architect, you the Master-builder: yours is the hand that shall erect the temple, when you shall bring to a selected place the fairest stones which you can finde, and cedar-wood hewed and shaped, so that you could raise towards heaven my Solomon's Palace, and nowhere be heard either ax, or hammer, or any instrument of iron, as you put them in place."

We would here say, returning to the "Sartor Resartus," that a secret relentless urging "Forward" seems to have been the true mainspring to the author's vast literary doings; and so p. 185, we have: "A nameless Unrest, says he, urged me forward; to which the outward motion was some momentary lying solace. Whither should I go? My Loadstars were blotted out; in that canopy of grim fire shone no star. Yet forward must I; the ground burnt under me; there was no rest for the sole of my foot. I was alone, alone! Ever too the strong inward longing shaped Fantasms for itself: towards these, one after the other, must I fruitlessly wander. A feeling I had that, for my fever-thirst, there was and must be somewhere a healing Fountain. To many fondly imagined Fountains, the Saints' Wells of these days, did I pilgrim; to great Men, to great Cities, to great Events: but found there no healing." A little further on he says: "Nevertheless still forward! I felt as if in great haste; to do I saw not what. From the depths of my own heart, it called to me, Forwards! The winds and the streams, and all Nature sounded to me, Forwards! *Ach Gott,* I was even, once for all, a Son of Time." His mission seems as if begirt by "the ring Necessity." See p. 121, 151 and 284. And on p. 134 he says; "I was like no other." See "Forward" our p. 149.

As to the author's early acquired ability to portray "characters," as spread into every phase of the writings under review, we, p. 143, quote thus:

"Nay from the chaos of that Library, I succeeded in fishing up more books perhaps than had been known to the very keepers thereof. The foundation of a Literary Life was hereby laid: I learned, on my own strength, to read fluently in almost all cultivated languages, on almost all subjects, and sciences; farther, as man is ever the prime object to man, already it was my favorite employment to read character in speculation, and from the Writing to construe the Writer. A certain groundplan of Human Nature and Life began to fashion itself in me; wondrous enough, now when I look back on it; for my whole Universe, physical and spiritual, was as yet a Machine!" Hence to Ophelia in the Play "whilst this machine is to him, Hamlet!" Note p. 163 "the mean clay-hamlets of Reality."

As to the author's early "Translations," see p. 153; and on p. 135 we have: "So much we can see; darkly, as through the foliage of some wavering thicket: a youth of no common endowment, who has passed happily through Childhood, less happily yet still vigorously through Boyhood, now at length perfect in 'dead vocables', and set down, as he hopes, by the living Fountain, there to superadd Ideas and Capabilities." His Mission, see our p. 24.

Turning now to the "Cypher Story" itself, touching "Translations" see p. 114, 118, 219, 220, and 313. From p. 118 we quote thus: "Besides the playes, three noteworthie translations are found in our workes, viz: Th' Iliad and Odyssey of Homer, and the Aeneid of Virgil, togather with a number of lesser workes of this sort, and a few short poemes. There is also the story, in verse, of th' Spanish Armada, and th' story of my owne life." See our p. 199.

Let the reader turn here to our "Defoe Period" p. 518, where will be found the same identical use of Capital Letters; and read attentively the Defoe paper on Pope's translation of Old Homer in relation to the "Spinners and Weavers." Then, as to these "Spinners and Weavers" let him read p. 312 and 313 of the "Sartor Resartus," and say, if he can; Carlyle was its author.

Now on p. 144 we have: "He appears, though in dreary enough humour, to be addressing himself to the Profession of Law;—whereof, indeed, the world has since seen him a public graduate." Note p. 136 to 144 what he says of his university days, and his views of the then English universities. Then see our p. 122.

We here turn to its Chapter on "Symbols;" and to Bacon's motives for concealment, and silence, in working out his vast posterity drama. Its second paragraph, p. 252 opens thus: "The benignant efficacies of Concealment, cries our Professor, who shall speak or sing? SILENCE and SECRECY! Altars might still be raised to them (were this an altar-building time) for universal worship. Silence is the element in which great things fashion themselves together; that at length they may emerge, full-formed and majestic, into the daylight of Life, which they are thenceforth to rule. Not William the Silent only, but all the considerable men I have known, and the most undiplomatic and unstrategic of these, forbore to babble of what they were creating and projecting. Nay, in thy own mean perplexities, do thou thyself but *hold thy tongue for one day:* on the morrow, how much clearer are thy purposes, and duties; what wreck and rubbish have those mute workmen within thee swept away, when intrusive noises were shut out!"

In the next paragraph we have: "Bees will not work except in darkness; Thought will not work except in Silence: neither will Virtue work except in Secrecy. Let not thy right hand know what thy left hand doeth! Neither shalt thou prate even to thy own heart of "those secrets known to all." Is not Shame the soil of all Virtue, of all good manners, and good morals? Like other plants, Virtue will not grow unless its root be hidden, buried from the eye of the sun. Let the sun shine on it, nay, do but look at it privily thyself, the root withers, and no flower will glad thee."

Note here Dark Authors, to be touched later.

A little further on we have: "Of kin to the so incalculable influences of Concealment, and connected with still greater things, is the wondrous agency of *Symbols.* In a Symbol there is concealment and yet revelation: here, therefore, by Silence and by Speech acting together, comes a doubled significance. And if both the Speech be itself high, and the Silence fit and noble, how expressive will their union be!" The genius which produced the "Pilgrim's Progress," was weaving here, reader. To Bacon's "Symbol Cypher" we have already made reference, p. 200.

Note, "Silence is the element in which great things fashion themselves together." As to the putting together of the parts of this anatomy, we, from the "Tale of a Tub" addressed to Posterity; using Everyman's Library edition of the work, on p. 81, have "To this end I have some time since, with a world of pains and art, dissected the carcase of human nature, and read many useful lectures upon the several parts, both containing and contained; till at last it smelt so strong I could preserve it no longer. Upon which I have been at great expense to fit up all the bones with exact contexture and in due symmetry; so that I am ready to show a very complete anatomy thereof to all curious gentlemen and others. But not to digress farther in the midst of a digression, as I have known some authors enclose digressions in one another like a nest of boxes, I do affirm that, having carefully cut up human nature, I have found a very strange, new, and important discovery, that the public good of mankind is performed by two ways, instruction and diversion." Note these "boxes" already referred to in the Cypher Story, p. 223 and see p. 211.

In our "Defoe Period" p. 573 and 549 to 589 we call "A Tale of a Tub" under careful review. On p. 549 to 554 note that it was a waif and how it came first to the press. It was a designed Ark to preserve learning. See our p. 120 to 123, and 142 to 146.

This work, now supposed Dean Swift's and addressed to "Prince Posterity" was also a waif from the Bacon budget. It was first put forth anonymously. It was not published as Swift's. It contains great subtlety. We have since our "Defoe Period," some new thoughts concerning it. How long after Bacon's fall was it written? See please p. 18, 20 and 27. Did it, in manuscript, contain the uncalled for use of capital letters? See p. 118 to 121. Note on p. 132 Bacon's distinctive use of the word "invention," where we have: "In my disposure of the employments of the brain I have thought fit to make invention the master, and to give method and reason the office of its lackeys." The "Sartor Resartus" was a later product. We show now how the clothes philosophy first took shape in the author's mind. In the "Tale of a Tub" p. 57 he says: "I have, with much pains and reading, collected out of ancient authors this short summary of a body of philosophy and divinity, which seems to have been composed by a vein and race of thinking very different from any other systems either ancient or modern. And it was not merely to entertain or satisfy the reader's curiosity, but rather to give him light into several circumstances of the following story; that, knowing the state of dispositions and opinions in an age so remote, he may better comprehend those great events which were the issue of them. I advise, therefore, the courteous reader to peruse with a world of application, again and again, whatever I have written upon the matter." See p. 5, 55 to 58 and 171.

Now the "Tale of a Tub" is presented as a work designed temporarily to avert unfavorable influences upon both church and state by reason of the already mentioned Hobbes' "Leviathan." See p. 33. Note then the "Leviathan" in Milton p. 14 and 155.

The "Tub" is designed to divert the whale, the "Leviathan," until other preparations can be made to protect the ship of state. The "Tub" presents the side of the church and literature; in the controversy, for reform; by using alternating Sections; leaving the work of protection, as to the state; until other plans can be perfected. The author's lash is aimed here, as in the other works, chiefly at Papists and Calvin, or the Presbyterians. See our p. 133, and 204.

After the words, "Popish plots" in Section 1, p. 52, there exists, we judge, a short, but most vile interpolation. The motive, now.

Referring in this Section itself p. 45 to Scotland; we have: "Of pulpits there are in this island several sorts; but I esteem only that made of timber from the *sylva Caledonia* (Scotland)." And see please p. 103, 120 to 130. King James 1st is referred to, we say, on p. 124 where we have: "He was also the first in these kingdoms who began to improve the Spanish accomplishment of braying."

In this work, the retailoring period of its own great author begins; and, first, with the church. Bacon's First period productions, including his Hobbes' "Leviathan," with its now offensive divine right of Kings doctrine, are to be weeded, retailored. This is to be effected by his "Classic Authors in Wood"—his own "Grubean Sages." In weeding matters which concern the State, the prose writings of Milton were chief, though handled by them all, especially by Defoe. See the Addison articles on matters of state, in Vol. 5.

In the work itself, p. 48 these Sages are called "the Grub Street brotherhood." We touch here the method devised for bringing forth the great scheme. The entire body of literary work is presented, as grounded upon three literary societies; "Gresham and Will's" being offshoots from the first. Those mentioned are said to be "seminaries not only of our planting, but our watering too." The two offspring societies are said to seek the ruin of the first. And those from the first, are said to desert to them. These three societies were to establish, we judge, the new Forum, the Club System, the new Seats of Learning of the Defoe period. See in this, please, p. 4, 48, 115 to 118 and 159.

In the great scheme, this permits "Gresham and Will's" to draw from, discuss, and retailor, works of the First period: and pour them thence into the new Forum; whereby the entire age freed from literary domination might become cultured upon every phase of human learning. See here, "The Battle of the Books," p. 143 to 169; and our p. 120 to 126.

Under subtle forms of entertainment, in the work, are couched the firmest truths. Whatever is satire, should be culled, placed and studied. King James 1st, was Scotch and Presbyterian, and is made to personate not only Calvin, or Jack; but minor religious sects. He is presented as having a foot in the same center with Peter, or the Church of Rome. See our p. 133. When will our instructors in English literature furnish forth an explanation of these works? Like the Sonnets, they have long defied interpretation.

On p. 49 the author claims there were grubean ages as well as sages. He says: "In consequence of these momentous truths the grubaean ages have always chosen to convey their precepts and their arts shut up within the vehicles of types and fables; which having been perhaps more careful and curious in adorning than was altogether necessary, it has fared with these vehicles, after the usual fate of coaches over-finely painted and gilt, that the transitory gazers have so dazzled their eyes and filled their imaginations with the outward lustre, as neither to regard or consider the person or the parts of the owner within." See "the republic of dark authors," p. 118; and what "dark" means.

And on p. 83 the author says: "I must needs own it was by the assistance of this arcanum that I, though otherwise *impar*, have adventured upon so daring an attempt, never achieved or undertaken before, but by a certain author called Homer; in whom, though otherwise a person not without some abilities, and, for an ancient, of a tolerable genius, I have discovered many gross errors, which are not to be forgiven his very ashes, if by chance any of them are left. For whereas we are assured he designed his work for a complete body of all knowledge, human, divine, political, and mechanic, it is manifest he has wholly neglected some, and been very imperfect in the rest." Let Sections 1, 5 and 7 be here read with care. Section 7, p. 93 opens thus: "I have sometimes heard of an Iliad in a nutshell; but it has been my fortune to have much oftener seen a nutshell in an Iliad. There is no doubt that human life has received most wonderful advantages from both; but to which of the two the world is chiefly indebted I shall leave among the curious as a problem worthy of their utmost inquiry." See Homer, our p. 225.

That Bacon was the restorer of ancient learning and the true ancient critic, see please Section 3 in full p. 63 to 71. See then p. 17 and 18 what is said of the already mentioned Duke of Buckingham; and the quarrel between the spider and the bee p. 9 and 10; and the now adverse criticism through Momus, and the downing of the author, p. 145 to 163. The mentioned "Horse I ride" in the "Sartor Resartus" will here be found at p. 18, 19, 119, 150, 156, 160 and 171.

Having so much yet to say, it is with regret, we assure the reader, that we here close the outlining of this great drama. Let it be done in the words Bacon puts into the mouth of his Addison Vol. 6, p. 582 concerning the mentioned Brotherhood, where we have:

"Now sing we whence the puppet-actors came,
  What hidden power supplies the hollow frame;
  What cunning agent o'er the scenes presides,
  And all the secret operation guides.
  The turner shapes the useless log with care,
  And forces it a human form to wear:
  With the sharp steel he works the wooden race,
  And lends the timber an adopted face.
  Tenacious wires the legs and feet unite,
  And arms connected keep the shoulders right.
  Adapted organs to fit organs join,
  And joints with joints, and limbs with limbs combine.
  Then adds he active wheels and springs unseen,
  By which he artful turns the small machine,
  That moves at pleasure by the secret wires;
  And last his voice the senseless trunk inspires.
  From such a union of inventions came,
  And to perfection grew, the puppet-frame;
  The workman's mark its origin reveal,
  And own the traces of the forming steel.
  Hence are its dance, its motions, and its tone,
  Its squeaking voice, and accents not its own."

Let the foregoing be called to direct relation, point by point, with Bacon's government model found at the opening of his "Leviathan," and with his words wherein he says: "I will instruct the actors and serve posterity."

INDEX

A

AIR, O ancient power of, p. 156. A permanent body; not compounded; a body through which all other bodies are seen, p. 156 to 158. Then 68 to 75. Its "middle regions" p. 171 to 174 and 211.

ASTRONOMY, Distinctive. Bacon's own system, p. 162 to 166, 171 to 174, 210 and 211.

ALLEGORY, "I did Pilgrim," p. 223 to 227; then 121 and 217; the "Pilgrim's Progress," p. 115, 135 to 138, 162, and 183 to 187.

ALPHABET, Nature's. Bacon's greatest discovery, p. 3, 7, 49, 51, 57, 66, 75, 107, 155, 172, 195 to 198, 200, 201, 206, 207, 218 to 223.

AREOPAGITICA, Protest against legal restraint upon authorship, p. 153 and 197.

ANONYMOUS, Writings. Defoe, p. 126 and 127. Addison, p. 142 and 143. Swift, p. 142, 208 and 227.

ALMANAC, Noted Bickerstaff papers and the almanac, p. 42 and 125.

B

BACON, Sir Francis. His Genesis, p. 7, 12, 13, 20, 23, 105, 193, 211, 213, 215 and 217.

BACON, The "sorry bookmaker." His own believed in covert mission, p. 3 to 6, 24, 58, 59, 111, 112, 121 to 124, 140, 142, 151 to 155, 168, 190, 200, and 222 to 232.

BACON, A concealed poet, p. 17 to 26, 80 to 87, 141, 153, 190 to 194.

BACON, A secret relentless urging "Forward" the mainspring to his vast literary doings, p. 24, 149 and 223 to 228.

BACON, And Alexander the Great. Doings contrasted by Bacon himself, p. 140, 152 and 222.

BACON, In his Milton, p. 155 to 190. In his "Sartor Resartus," p. 192 to 228. In his Cypher Work, p. 197 to 225. In his "Tub;" his Ark to preserve learning, p. 123, 141 to 143 and 227 to 232.

BACON, Sir Francis. His Shakespeare Sonnets. Their two Sentinels. These double—lock the door, p. 7, 26, 47, and 81 to 87. Reasons for their use, p. 39. Numbering blurs Sonnet relations, p. 9, 10, and 33. Collating them into related parts, "Our Door of Entrance," p. 12 to 16.

1. PART 1, Concerns Queen Elizabeth and her successor, p. 7, 10, and 20 to 22 and 151. Their author's struggle with her royal "Will," p. 13 and 21 to 24.

2. KING JAMES, and the author's self-told overthrow, p. 8 to 11, and 27 to 45; then 87 to 92, and 102 to 109, 123. The noted Overbury trial, and the King, p. 28, and 90 to 96.
3. THE AUTHOR'S wonder, p. 56 and 57. His tabular system of philosophy, p. 48 to 80. Its eternized tables, p. 62 to 75. Its "blessed key," p. 5, 64, 67, 68, and 75 to 79; then 66 to 75, 155 to 157 and 190.
4. THE AUTHOR'S "noted weed," of the Sonnets, and its laudation, p. 13, 14, 57, 80 to 87, 150 and 217. His pronoun cover words used in them, p. 9, 10, 14 to 16, 82, 148 and 194.
New life "on second head" by the author, p. 10, 105 to 110, 113, 129 and 222 to 230.

BACON, Overthrow told now in facts of history, p. 28 to 30, 36 to 39, 41 to 46, 59; then 90 to 105, 109, 110, and 123. The Trap, Bacon within it, p. 37, 41 to 46, 94, 95, 98, 103, 104, 108 and 109.

C

CYPHERS, Those made use of by Bacon, p. 200. "My last contrivance," p. 87, 102, 129, 192, 195 to 198, 201, 202, 217.
Deciphered work, p. 197, 199, 204, 206, 207, 211 to 214, 217, 219 to 225. See then p. 51 to 54.
CHARACTERS, Ability to portray them, p. 124 and 224.
CROMWELL, His party the Independents, and their aims, p. 129 to 135, 137, 143 to 146, 204 and 229.

D

DUTY, Duty and passive obedience, p. 29, 30, 45 and 205. Cultured roots, p. 215.
DOMINATION, Both literary and ecclesiastic, p. 119 to 127. Fold broken from, p. 119 and 120.
DEFOE period. Involves it no mystery? p. 125, 144, 196, 207 and 208.
DREAMS—Visions. They disclose ideational possibilities, p. 182, 192; then 182 and 204.

E

ENIGMAS, The title-page to the Shakespeare Sonnets, p. 26 and 83. To the Plays, p. 198. The Epitaph, p. 86. The Monument, p. 84. The author's own monument, p. 45, 107 to 114.
ENVY, Ever at the door of him who thinks himself wise, p. 24.
EVIL, The knowledge of. Its value to him who would be the true instructor, with Bacon's views, p. 113 to 117 and 139. Knowledge, the only true fence, against evil, p. 115.

INDEX

ENTERTAINMENT, No valued culture without it, p. 6, 113, and 115 to 118, 120, 183 and 193.

EARTH, The mother of nature. Pendulous. Self-balanced. Her womb and tomb, p. 163, and 165 to 174.

F

FORMS, God only the Architect of, p. 57. They, as "surds," represent the laws, "the simple natures" that compose Bacon's great "Alphabet," p. 3 to 6; then 49, 196 to 199 and 220. Found only by "Tables of Discovery," p. 49, 50, 65 to 80, and 201.

FORMULA, The Key; the only door to Bacon's system, p. 51, 68, 75, 155, 197, 199, and 207.

G

GIFTS, Bacon's mental, p. 6, 110 to 114, 119, 145, 154, 161, 194 and 200. See "The Gifted," p. 146 to 151.

GARMENT, The Tailor's Art, p. 76, 193, 195, 209 and 212.

GOVERNMENT, Bacon's model and writings, p. 4, 100 to 102, 119, 132 to 136, 137 to 140, 143 to 145, 146 to 152, 180, 185, 187, 203 to 206, 208 to 211 and 228 to 230.

H

HIGHGATE, Bacon, and the Hague, p. 127 to 129, 145 and 218.

HARLEY, Sir Robert and Bacon's "cabinets, boxes and presses." He the financial movement behind the manuscripts, p. 7, 113, 118, 127, ·129 and 202.

HISTORY, Bacon's Natural. Like no other, p. 50, 51, 57, 64, 73 and 74. This "the bosom to philosophy." The "New Organ," from that bosom was to draw "nature's sweet milk," p. 74.

I

INTELLIGENCE, Instinctive, Ideational, Creative, p. 159; and "the discourse of reason," p. 158.

INVENTION, The Master, p. 50, 55, 70 and 228.

INSTAURATION, Bacon's. Its different parts, p. 51, 64 to 66.

J

JEWELS, Bacon's, p. 28, 68, 77 to 79, and 201.

K

KNOWLEDGE, The true Baconian mark, p. 68.

KING, Charles 1st; and the noted army prayer meeting in 1648, where his death was resolved upon, p. 137 to 139, and 180.

L

LEARNING, Bacon's advancement and new seats of, p. 25, 120, 123 to 128 and 227 to 232. These the new Forum, p. 119, 120, 121, 141 to 146, and 230. Their structure, the nurse to his own thoughts, as well as to others, p. 120, 122 and 125.

LIGHT, Its origin, p. 74, 75, 154 to 156, and 161.

LOVE. Love and lust, and their effects, as spread throughout these writings, p. 116.

LITERATURE. English. And "the good pens that forsake me not," p. 6, 44, 112, 151 and 202.

M

MAGIC, Persian. Bacon's knowledge of, touching both government and philosophy, p. 209 to 211, and 217.

METAPHYSICS. In metaphysics Bacon differs from all others, p. 154, 191 and 192.

MYTHOLOGY, Bacon's in his Milton, p. 170 to 190. In other works, p. 140 to 142, 170, 174, 176, 183, and 193.

MYTHUS, The new, p. 4, 132, 135, 154, 193, 208, 213 to 216, 218 to 222, 229; or the collated "host of divine works" mentioned at p. 4. See p. 98.

MANUSCRIPTS, Undated, misplaced, tampered with, garbled, p. 44, 61, 67, 68, 73, 103, 111, 122 to 124, 126 and 145.

MYSTERIES, The Hebrew; the sciences, the Alphabet, p. 49, 174, 179, 183, 186, 193, and 196.

N

NATURE. God's Art. Her key, her apex, the human body, p. 3, 156, 203, 208, 224 to 232. Heat and cold, her two hands, p. 172. Her contending grounds "the middle regions" of the air, p. 172 to 174 and 211. Her warriors; "Hot, Cold, Moist and Dry," p, 170 to 174, 218 and 220. Earth, her womb and tomb, p. 163, 169 and 171.

O

OBEDIENCE, Duty and obedience cultured roots from the outset, p. 29, 30, 45, 99, 104, 205 and 215.

P

PHILOSOPHY, Bacon's. Is tabular. It differs from all others, p. 3 to 6, and 48 to 80. So distinctive is it, as not to be contrasted even, with those extant, p. 71 to 75. Its critics unjust, p. 50, 61, 71 to 74, 79 and 200. It can be opened only by means of a key. It was structured for an Interpreter, p. 50, 51, 57, 64, 67, 164,

165, 185, 199, 201 and 218. It was not designed to take the place of existing methods, p. 52; but for a secret order, "The Sons of Science" of his "New Atlantis," p. 67, 95, 99, 100, 104, 117, to 120, 143, 151, 154 and 199. Confused by undated misplaced parts, p. 67 to 71.

R

REFORM. Bacon's vast literary carcass, p. 119, 124, 125, 139 to 142, 154 197 and 203. Its never before attempted method of introduction, p. 6, 208, 228 to 232. Was secretary, not merely to Cromwell and the Independents, p. 144 and 145; but to "His Royal Highness Prince Posterity," by aid of that evolved "Brotherhood," his "Classic Authors in Wood," p. 142, 194, 195 and 229.

S

SOUL. Its outer walls. Its fading mansion, p. 137 and 192.

SUBSTANCE. Distinctive views by Bacon touching substance, colors and light, p. 61, 67 to 71, 74 to 76, 155 to 159, 170, 192 to 194, 213 and 214.

SATAN. The deeps of, should be all known to him who would be the true instructor with Bacon's views, p. 6, 114 to 116, 139 to 141 and 176.

T

TEUFELSDROCKH, Prof. T., and Queen Elizabeth's apron; and the little piece of Persian silk that covered his baby face in the Basket, when first viewed by his foster parents, p. 211, 213 and 217.

TRANSLATIONS. Early work, p. 224 to 226.

U

UNIVERSITIES. Bacon's views concerning these seats of learning, p. 119 to 123 and 225.

V

VOCABULARY. Bacon's throughout the writings here called under review, p. 46, 47, 119, 125, 146, 187 and 202. The law of his words, see p. 116 to 119.

W

WAIFS. The Carlyle, from the Bacon Budget; some of them woefully garbled, p. 130 to 134, 138, 146 to 151, 152, 193, 216 and 225. Other waifs, p. 137, 142, 143, 145 and 227.

C 49 89

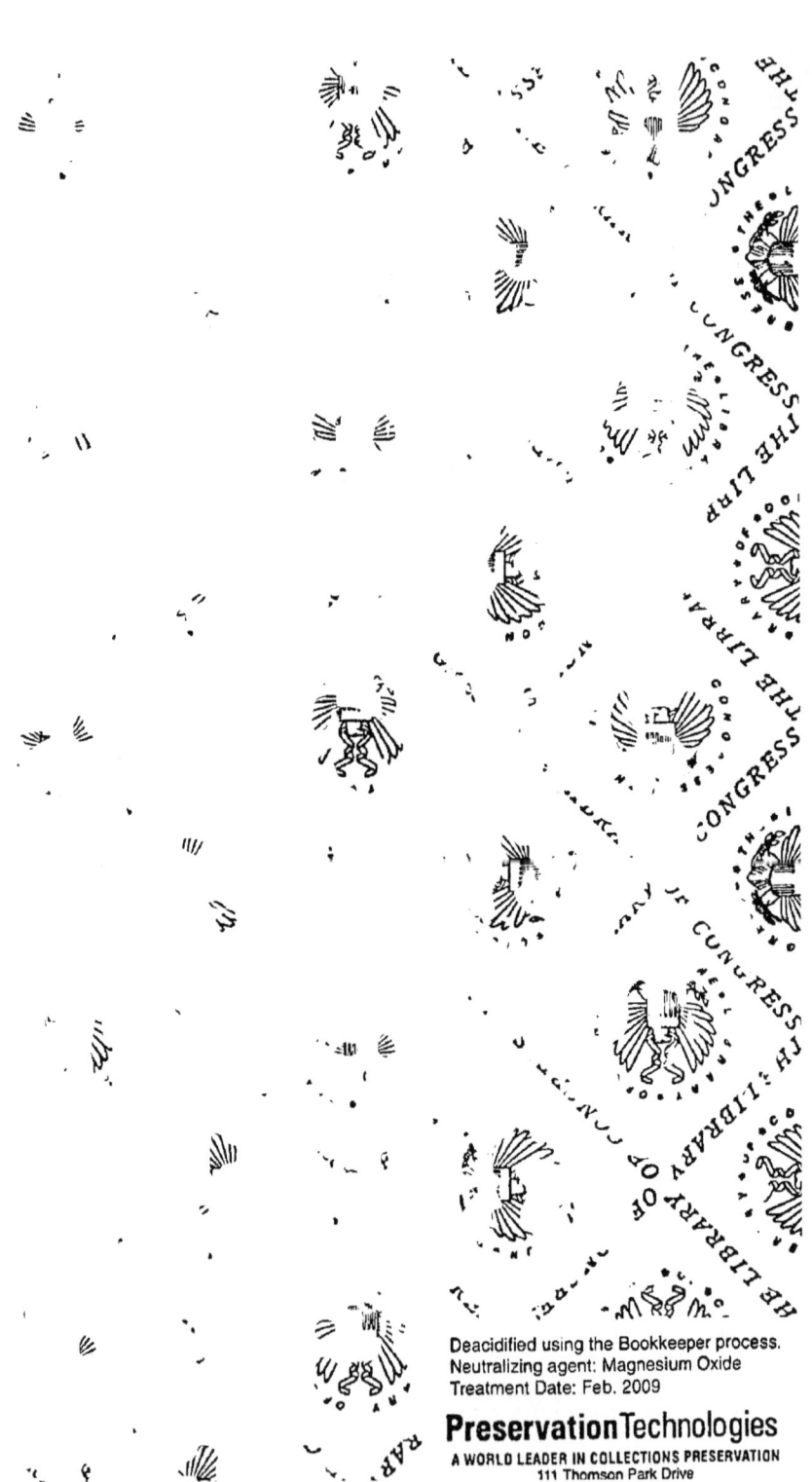

Deacidified using the Bookkeeper process.
Neutralizing agent: Magnesium Oxide
Treatment Date: Feb. 2009

PreservationTechnologies
A WORLD LEADER IN COLLECTIONS PRESERVATION
111 Thomson Park Drive